THE LANE CENTER SERIES
VOLUME 4

SPRING 2016

ISLAM AT JESUIT COLLEGES AND UNIVERSITIES

Published by the
UNIVERSITY OF SAN FRANCISCO PRESS
Joan and Ralph Lane Center
for Catholic Studies and Social Thought

University of San Francisco
2130 Fulton Street
San Francisco, CA 94117-1080
www.usfca.edu/lane-center

Collection copyright © 2016 | ISBN 978-1-944769-13-0

Authors retain the copyright to their individual essays. Queries regarding permissions should be sent to the authors using the email addresses provided with their essays.

Published by the University of San Francisco Press through the Joan and Ralph Lane Center for Catholic Studies and Social Thought of the University of San Francisco.

The Lane Center Series promotes the center's mission to advance the scholarship and application of the Catholic intellectual tradition in the church and society with an emphasis on social concerns. The series features essays by Lane Center scholars, guest speakers, and USF faculty. It serves as a written archive of Lane Center events and programs and allows the work of the center to reach a broader audience.

THE LANE CENTER SERIES
VOLUME 4

SPRING 2016

ISLAM AT JESUIT COLLEGES AND UNIVERSITIES

UNIVERSITY OF SAN FRANCISCO | Joan and Ralph Lane Center for Catholic Studies and Social Thought

TABLE OF CONTENTS

INTRODUCTION
Aysha Hidayatullah

―――――――

**JESUIT HISTORY, MISSION AND IDENTITY:
JESUITS AND THE INTERRELIGIOUS COMMITMENTS OF VATICAN II**
John Borelli

―――――――

STUDYING AND TEACHING ISLAM: DIFFERENT EXPERIENCES
Patrick J. Ryan, S.J.

―――――――

**THE CHALLENGE AND THE PROMISE OF
TEACHING ISLAM AT A JESUIT UNIVERSITY**
Umeyye Isra Yazicioglu

―――――――

**WHERE WE HAVE BEEN, WHERE WE ARE GOING:
SOME REFLECTIONS ON THE PAST, PRESENT,
AND FUTURE OF JESUIT/MUSLIM RELATIONS**
Paul Shore

―――――――

**ISSUES OF IMMEDIACY AND IDENTITY IN SCHOLARSHIP
AND PEDAGOGY FOR ISLAM IN THE ACADEMY**
Martin Nguyen

―――――――

Table of Contents (cont.)

The Future of Muslims in Jesuit Universities
Thomas Michel, S.J.

The Future of Islam at Jesuit Universities
Amir Hussain

INTRODUCTION

AYSHA HIDAYATULLAH

Over the course of my nearly eight years as a professor of Islamic studies at the University of San Francisco (USF), I have developed a deep appreciation for the gift of teaching and researching Islam at an educational institution grounded in the Jesuit Catholic values of serving justice and the common good. I am greatly moved by the generosity and openness with which I have been welcomed by a Jesuit university to contribute to the study of religion and entrusted with the spiritual formation of students here as a Muslim and scholar of Islam. I have come to see the opportunity to develop Islamic studies, and in particular to teach Islam as part of our undergraduate Theology and Religious Studies core curriculum, as a profound privilege and responsibility.

Quite soon after my arrival at USF in 2008, I began hearing of the marked increase of Muslim students at U.S. Catholic colleges and universities generally, and taking note of the critical mass of scholars of Islam being hired by Jesuit colleges and universities specifically. I wondered how my Islamic studies colleagues at other Jesuit schools saw their work in relation to the Jesuit missions of their institutions, and how the growing engagement with Islam and Muslims was

---

Aysha Hidayatullah is Associate Professor in the Department of Theology and Religious Studies at the University of San Francisco, where she teaches courses on Islam, gender, race, and ethics. She received her M.A. and Ph.D. in Religious Studies from the University of California, Santa Barbara. She is the author of *Feminist Edges of the Qur'an* (Oxford University Press) and currently serves as Co-Chair for the Islam, Gender, Women Group of the American Academy of Religion.

impacting our schools broadly. It seemed to me that a conference to address these topics collectively was in order. In early 2014 a crucial conversation with Professor Amir Hussain of Loyola Marymount University provided the necessary encouragement and contacts to begin imagining such a gathering practically. Within a few months of reaching out to others—including a number of esteemed scholars who have contributed centrally to historic developments in Muslim-Christian relations over the past decades—I was delighted by the support and enthusiasm expressed by faculty and staff at fellow Jesuit institutions whom I invited to come together at USF.

On April 10-11, 2015 the University of San Francisco hosted the national conference, "Islam at U.S. Jesuit Colleges and Universities." Along with dozens of faculty, staff, and students from USF, the event gathered about 75 attendees from other institutions. Altogether the group represented 24 of the 28 U.S. Jesuit colleges and universities (as well as a few non-Jesuit institutions). The overall aim of the conference was to examine the evolution of the mission, objectives, and identity of Catholic Jesuit colleges and universities in light of the expansion of the study of Islam and the growing presence of Muslim faculty, staff, and students on our campuses. Together we examined some of the theological implications of supporting Islamic studies as part of Jesuit education, as well as possibilities and challenges of Christian-Muslim encounters at Jesuit institutions.

The conference was structured around two keynote addresses on "The Future of Islam at Jesuit Colleges and Universities" by Amir Hussain and Thomas Michel, S.J., as well as four roundtable discussions on the topics of: "Jesuit History, Mission, and Identity" (led by speakers Patrick Ryan, S.J., Daniel Madigan, S.J., John Borelli, and Paul Shore); "Comparative Theology" (led by speakers Yvonne Haddad, Jack Renard, Irfan Omar, and Umeyye Isra Yazicioglu); "Teaching, Curricula, and Educational Resources" (led by speakers Marcia Hermansen, Jim Morris, Kathryn Kueny, and Martin Nguyen); and "Student Life, Community Outreach, and International Networks" (led by speakers Yahya Hendi, Zeki Saritoprak, Achmat Salie, and Lulu Santana). A Friday Muslim Jumʻah prayer service was led by Abu

Qadir Al-Amin, a local San Francisco imam, with multi-faith prayer and halal meal accommodations provided throughout the conference.

On the one-year anniversary of the conference, I am pleased that this issue of the *Lane Center Series* features a selection of the talks given at the conference. This issue consists of the written (and in some cases somewhat abbreviated) versions of the remarks delivered by the 7 of the 18 speakers at the conference who were able to submit them for publication. Their talks served as starting points for longer discussions involving all conference attendees collectively. Thus, this issue provides a partial but valuable record of the territory covered by the event over both days.

In the remarks collected in this issue, John Borelli points to the broader context of the conference's inquiries by surveying the history of important steps in Catholic-Muslim relationships and Catholic/Jesuit commitments to interreligious dialogue with Muslims. Patrick Ryan, S.J., discusses his experiences teaching Islam as a Jesuit both inside and outside the U.S., and highlights his efforts to foster the development of "trialogue" (Jewish-Christian-Muslim dialogue). Umeyye Isra Yazicioglu observes how teaching religion at a Jesuit institution facilitates authentic and meaningful discussions of faith, and looks forward to the collaboration of Christians and Muslims in this setting to articulate the relevance of faith to one's self-positioning in the world. Paul Shore suggests that the curiosity and conversation engendered by studying the history of Jesuit-Muslim interaction since the founding of the Society of Jesus—in moments of both tension and receptivity—can furnish important starting points for mutual exchange between Muslims and Christians in Jesuit institutions. Martin Nguyen addresses the challenges of teaching Islam in the post-9/11 era, particularly the demands of responding to current events related to Islam/Muslims. He also presents the possibility of Jesuit colleges and universities supporting the development of constructive theology by Muslims. In his keynote address, Thomas Michel, S.J., discusses his courses on Muslim-Christian relations and Biblical literature at Georgetown University's campus in Qatar, where most of the student body is Muslim. He observes that the interfaith encounters there, both inside and outside the classroom, speak to Jesuit educational values that support students from diverse backgrounds learning to live together, called to that task by the faith commitments and common missions of Christians and Muslims. Finally, in his keynote address Amir Hussain weaves the story of how he came to the study of religion and snapshots of the history of Muslims in North America together with his reflections on how Muslims and Christians might cooperate toward common goals, including through the comparative study of religion and development of Islamic theology at Jesuit colleges and universities, as a way of moving forward together with the language of love.

I am grateful to USF's Joan and Ralph Lane Center for Catholic Studies and Social Thought (also a generous sponsor of the conference itself) for providing an ideal medium for archiving the material in this volume and thereby recognizing its significance in terms of the development of Jesuit education and dialogue; to Erin Brigham for her brilliant editorial work; to Jacquelyn Tran for her patient help with transcription; Kim Connor and Mike Duffy for their encouragement of this volume; and Monica Doblado for her tireless organizational assistance.

An archive of full-length videos of all conference talks and other information about the conference is permanently accessible through the conference website: http://www.usfca.edu/arts-sciences/research/islam-jesuit-colleges-universities.

JESUIT HISTORY, MISSION AND IDENTITY:

JESUITS AND THE INTERRELIGIOUS COMMITMENTS OF VATICAN II

JOHN BORELLI

When I first studied the documents of General Congregation 34 of 1995, when the Jesuits made their important commitment to interreligious dialogue, I was struck by how they framed that commitment. They declared interreligious dialogue would be

John Borelli is the Coordinator for Interreligious Dialogue and Mission for the Jesuit Conference of Canada and the United States and has served as the Special Assistant for Interreligious Initiatives to the President of Georgetown University since 2004. Before that, he was Associate Director of the Secretariat for Ecumenical and Interreligious Affairs at the U. S. Conference of Catholic Bishops for 16 years and Interim Director from 2001-2002 and a consultor to the Vatican's Pontifical Council for Interreligious Dialogue from 1990 to 2007. He taught full-time at Fordham University (Ph.D, 1976, history of religions and theology) during his final year of graduate studies and for 11 years at the College of Mount St. Vincent (New York City), and has published over 200 articles in the past 30 years on the history of religions and ecumenical and interreligious dialogue and relations.

henceforth central to their mission as a Society in service to the mission of the church. At that time, twenty years ago, the Jesuits drew attention to significant developments at Vatican II (1962-1965) as well as developments in subsequent papal teaching. They acknowledged the long history of Jesuit engagement in interreligious understanding from the time of the first Jesuits in the sixteenth century, but they also pointed out the importance of the documents of Vatican II in re-ordering the church's priorities as a whole. That re-ordering can be expressed in a single word: "dialogue."[1]

I have focused a good part of my research during the past nine years on the conciliar act that most clearly had something to say about the future of Islam at Jesuit colleges and universities. That conciliar act was the *Declaration on the Relation of the Church to Non-Christian Religions*. It is recognized more briefly by its Latin title from its first two words, *Nostra aetate*, "in our time" or "in our age." This shortest of all the documents of Vatican II, and probably the most controversial, is truly a window on the council. There was no single line of development from the original suggestion in June, 1960 that the council could facilitate, in some way, relations with Jews, to the final declaration in 1965 that accomplished so much more. Jesuit Cardinal Augustin Bea, then president of the Secretariat for the Promotion of Christian Unity, liked to use the metaphor of the tiny mustard seed of a brief suggestion about the church's teaching on the Jews that grew into a tree large enough for the followers of all the religions on its branches.[2] The final document addressed the unity of the human family, the ancient questions we humans continue to face about our destiny and ultimate meaning, and the role of religions and their interactions in answering these profound questions. It also discussed the church's relations with the followers of other religions, particularly with Muslims and with Jews, and stated the church's absolute rejection of all forms of discrimination.

Many Jesuits participated in Vatican II, some as bishops, and probably most of those were from Catholic missions. At least one of these missionary bishops had survived Dachau, Adam Kozłowiecki, archbishop of Lusaka at the time of the council. Other Jesuits served as *periti* or theological experts. Karl Rahner, Henri de Lubac, and

John Courtney Murray stand out among these. There were Jesuits who staffed commissions and secretariats for the council. One of these, Brooklyn-born John Francis Long, served on the staff of the Secretariat for Promoting Christian Unity, the body that was responsible for *Nostra aetate*. Fr. Long, who was a mentor to me on Vatican II and ecumenism, and even a little on *Nostra aetate*, had the task of gathering four experts on Islam to compose a paragraph on why Catholics should respect Muslims and how Catholics and Muslims might cooperate in the future. This was on October 9, 1964, at a crucial time in the history of the declaration.

With faith and hope, Fr. Long gathered two Missionaries of Africa, Robert Caspar and Joseph Cuoq, along with Jean Corbon, a diocesan priest and a former Missionary of Africa, and Georges Anawati, a Dominican. At the time, these four and Fr. Long, much less the members of the Secretariat, did not know where their paragraph would go. An effort was underway to submarine the expanding draft on the Jews and other non-Christians and let its fragments be scattered among other conciliar texts. Despite all the intrigue that flowed through the council during the month of October in 1964, these four, under Fr. Long's leadership, composed the lines that eventually became the approved passage representing an important beginning in Catholic-Muslim relations:

> The Church regards with esteem also the Muslims. They adore the one God, who is living and subsisting in himself, merciful and all-powerful, the Creator of heaven and earth, (Cf. S. Greg. VII, Letter III, 21 to Anzir [Al-Nāṣir], king of Mauritania: ed. E. Caspar in MGH, ep. sel. II, 1920, I, p. 288, 11, 15; PL 148, 451A.) who has spoken to humans; they strive to submit wholeheartedly even to His inscrutable decrees, just as Abraham, with whom the faith of Islam is gladly linked, submitted to God. Though they do not acknowledge Jesus as God, they revere him as a prophet. They also honor Mary, his virgin mother; at times they even call on her with devotion. Moreover, they look forward to the day of judgment when God will reward all those raised up. For this reason, they value the moral life and worship God, especially through prayer, almsgiving and fasting.

In the course of centuries there have indeed arisen not a few quarrels and hostilities between Christians and Muslims. But now this Sacred Synod pleads with all to forget the past, to make sincere efforts for mutual understanding, and so to work together for the preservation and fostering of social justice, moral welfare, and peace and freedom, for all humankind.[3]

When reading these lines today, one can easily see how they were only meant as a starting point. While they offer very important comments, they do not say enough for our contemporary concerns and interests. They constitute only one beginning, one among many beginnings associated with Vatican II. Pope Paul VI publically addressed Muslims for the first time in a pastoral way from Bethlehem on January 6, 1964. This address was a first in some ways. Later that year, in his encyclical on the church in dialogue, *Ecclesiam suam*, Paul VI would write about Muslims: "We do well to admire these people for all that is good and true in their worship of God." This, too, was a first for a major teaching document of the Catholic Church.

In addition to those experts helping with the paragraph on Muslims, two Jesuits helped with the rest of *Nostra aetate*—Josef Neuner, who was living in India and had accompanied the Indian bishops to Rome, and Paul Pfister, likewise for Japan. They provided much of the initial draft of the first two paragraphs of *Nostra aetate*. The expanded text with additions by Neuner, Pfister, and Long received overwhelming approval as a draft for further emendations in November 1964 as the third of the four periods of the council came to a close. Two Jesuits, Joseph Masson (Louvain) and Piet Fransen (Innsbruck), presented two of the four papers at a small conference that Josef Neuner organized in Bombay at the end of that same month in 1964 preceding the December visit of Pope Paul VI. The topic of the meeting was "Christian Revelation and World Religions." Another Jesuit quite active at Vatican II, Jean Danièlou, objected mightily when he read about the conference in *Le Monde*. Danièlou was very displeased with the expanded draft because it made Christianity just one among all religions. Dominican Yves Congar already alerts us to Danièlou's problem with a journal entry in October 1964. There were Jesuits with opposing opinions throughout these developments.[4]

However, there seems to have been little direct Jesuit influence on the paragraph on Muslims, despite Jesuits having run Baghdad College since 1932, their St. Joseph University having roots in Beirut from 1875, and their long history of working elsewhere in the Middle East and South Asia. A Spanish Jesuit, Felix Pareja Casañas, had even been teaching Islam or "Islamology," as he called it, at the Gregorian University in Rome through the 1950s. During this same time, Jesuit Vincent Courtois published a quarterly from Calcutta, "Notes on Islam." These two and other Jesuits connected with a few international initiatives in the 1950s—all very preliminary and not unrelated to sponsored activities during the Cold War—provided a cadre ready to implement whatever new directions for cooperation with Muslims that the council might encourage. The important Jesuit weekly, *La Civiltà Cattolica*, wanted a four-part series on Islam and contemporary events in the 1950s, especially addressing the struggle against communism. The Jesuit editor chose Wilhelm De Vries, a fellow Jesuit and a specialist in Oriental Christianity, to write the series. De Vries, who taught at the Pontifical Oriental Institute in Rome, published the following articles:

"La Potenza Mondiale dell'Islam, Oggi." *La Civiltà Cattolica* 1957/II, 121-131.
"Qual è la Situazione presente del Mondo Islamico?" 1957/III, 127-137.
"Progressivo Adattamento dei Musulmani ai Sistemi Europei." 1957/III, 365-376.
"L'Isam è un Baluardo contro il Comunismo?" 1957/IV, 263-273.

Even before Vatican II ended, the Jesuits were holding General Congregation 31 and re-prioritizing the Society. The first segment met May-July 1965, almost exactly fifty years ago, before the final period of the council. Would they have believed anyone who suggested to them meeting in May 1965 that fifty years later in April 2015, a conference on the future of Islam at Jesuit Colleges and Universities would attract 75 participants from all over the United States? It would have likely been a surprise even to a Society that is used to planning dramatically.

Jesuit representatives returned in 1966 and finished their General Congregation 31. In Decree 24 on mission service, there is mention of dialogue with non-Christian religions. This comes at the end of a list of works now more urgent and more universal due to Vatican II. The list in paragraph 430 reads: cooperation in the formation of clergy, religious, the laity for the apostolate, use of communications media, social apostolate, ecumenical work, and dialogue with non-Christian religions. Decree 26 welcomes and gives filial devotion to the commitment to ecumenism, admits sins against unity of Christians in Jesuit history, and asks for ecumenical education of Jesuits. When we read these statements today and other documents of that time, they seem cautious, like the important acts of Vatican II; yet they recommended structures that would bring about major progress. The same decree mentions "non-Christians" in the context of ecumenism, arguing in paragraph 462 that the common witness of Christians through ecumenism will shine among them and cause less scandal through division. The decree also discusses common problems that arise from relations with other religions.[5]

The Congress of Jesuit Ecumenists began meeting almost immediately after Vatican II because there was a healthy number of Jesuit scholars, theologians, and pastoral leaders committed to Christian unity. Ecumenism was safer and drew larger numbers. The congress met regularly in the post-Vatican II years. This is something obvious to us in the United States if we recall the makeup of our country at that time. There was little interest in interreligious relations beyond Jewish relations, for which *Nostra aetate* was originally conceived and as a result of which many Jewish groups were happy. Bishops in our dioceses could meet and form friendships with the chief rabbi in town. The United States had the largest Jewish population of any country after the war, and U.S. Jewish agencies lobbied heavily during the council for *Nostra aetate*. There were few opportunities then for a U.S. bishop to meet a chief imam. Interreligious work, especially relations with Muslims in North America and Europe, took a back seat to Jewish relations, really until the 1990s, despite a string of international developments affecting American life. Overwhelmingly in this context ecumenical work was seen as more central to theological and pastoral concerns than any kind of interreligious work.

When I arrived at Fordham University in the fall of 1968 for graduate study in theology, Thomas Berry, a Passionist, had the only doctoral program functioning at a Catholic University where one could engage in the history of religions within the context of theological studies. By the 1970s, his section had grown in popularity as the other traditional sections were decreasing in numbers. When I received my doctorate in 1976, the authorities at Fordham, many of whom were Jesuits, still believed that interreligious study, as it related to theological studies and the history of religions, was a passing fad, and therefore did not wish to strengthen the program. Eventually it was demoted to a master's level of study, but fortunately, by that time Boston College and other schools were beginning to develop competent programs. Here one can observe the struggle simply to keep a lively program of the history of religions alongside theological study alive at a Jesuit university, much less a program in Islamic studies. While we lacked expertise in Islamic studies at Fordham, it could be found in its metropolitan New York environment.

In 1987, I shifted away from academic life to a position at the U. S. Conference of Catholic Bishops in interreligious dialogue. This was more than twenty years after Vatican II, when I was the first full-time staff responsible for interreligious work. While I was also responsible for some ecumenical work, the bishops who funded my position along with the support staff and program money wanted me to begin a program in Catholic-Muslim relations. I devoted much of my time to developing a strategy which was multi-layered, involving education of diocesan personnel, forming friendships with Muslim leaders while developing a rapport with various organizations, entering and maintaining networks of expertise, and addressing questions and concerns arising from current events. After trial and error, some success, and years of building trust, a model to engage a broad network of partnerships in a convenient and inexpensive way emerged, which I termed "regional dialogues." By September 11, 2001, three regional dialogues were meeting regularly on an annual basis with focused agendas and commitment. We already had a rapport with Muslim leaders to face the new challenges from the attacks that day.

We also had developed a sound set of relations with African American Muslims who organized themselves around the person of Warith Deen Muhammad. Actually, in October 1999, at an interreligious service on the steps of St. Peter's Basilica in Rome concluding an interreligious assembly in preparation for the great jubilee year 2000, Warith Deen Muhammad, an African-American, was the first Muslim to pray alongside the pope in the Vatican itself. Our regional dialogues represented a phase in the development of the American Muslim community and the history of Christian-Muslim relations in the United States. These dialogues drew from academic expertise, but they were not precisely the kinds of projects one encounters on university campuses. We had joined with universities for academic style projects, but the dialogues jointly sponsored with Muslims were broader in focus than the engagement of academic subjects.

I can recall when Jesuit Francis Clooney, then on the faculty at Boston College, contacted me in 1999, about a year after General Congregation 34, seeking my advice on how Jesuits might implement in the United States their commitment to interreligious dialogue. I even saved a copy of my reply to him, where I had made suggestions that contrasted with the newly developing regional dialogues. My suggestion focused on the fact that there are 28 Jesuit colleges and universities in the United States and that "the Catholic Church in the next millennium will need a new generation of scholars who, competent in the essentials of theological study, have specialized in the study of various religious traditions." I also suggested annual symposia, visiting professorships, and an annual award for or lecture on interreligious activity in the Society. I also suggested various ways of networking among Jesuits and those at Jesuit institutions, a newsletter, directory, and annual communications.

I had little knowledge of how Frank implemented his task assigned by the U.S. Jesuit Conference until I left the Bishops' Conference in 2003 to take up my present position at Georgetown. Before my first day, Frank contacted me with the suggestion that I relieve him of the task. He had taken the important first steps and had provided an initial organization and networking. After a few months, the Jesuit Conference and Georgetown agreed to a Memorandum of Understanding that has been renewed every three years. It was last renewed in 2013. This present phase is an interim period in my mind, between the first few years under Frank as a beginning phase and the next phase of deeper commitment and implementation. We need to identify specific suggestions for this next phase.

The 28 colleges and universities are only a portion of the institutions in the United States with a Jesuit mission. There are many more high schools, parishes, retreat houses, formation houses, and a handful of special institutions, including migration and refugee services and volunteer corps. At colleges and universities, we find specialists in the study of various religions. One of the questions we face is—how do we maintain or grow that expertise at Jesuit colleges and universities while at the same time reaching all aspects of Jesuit life and completing the mission of all these other institutions? An increasing number of laypersons and priests associated with Jesuit institutions are formed in Ignatian practice through the exercises, retreats, and various prayer and reflection groups. As the number of Jesuits decrease, this formation of lay and ordained associates becomes increasingly important too for maintaining the character of a Jesuit institution.

My sense is that the exploration of the Ignatian character of dialogue, what we might call "the Ignatian charism for dialogue," has five components that reach these various kinds of Jesuit works and activities: an educational piece, a spiritual formation piece, a pastoral piece, a friendship or spiritual companionship piece, and a communication piece that includes a website.

Dialogue, my single word capturing the whole of this commitment, is not a subject but an orientation. It involves being "religious interreligiously," an expression used at General Congregation 34. In the past, Jesuits excelled in formation through the exercises, shaping a society of men concerned about the common good, justice, and the betterment of society as a whole. In their first two centuries, they excelled principally through their schools, humanistic in orientation, training the leaders of civil society to be good citizens and good men of faith. After the suppression and the restoration in 1814, in their attempt to recapture their network of educational institutions, Jesuits in the United States excelled in developing their network of colleges and universities with supporting high schools. John O'Malley, in the recent issue of *Studies in the Spirituality of Jesuits,* has shown how Jesuit education in its various incarnations has helped students: 1) expand beyond their present experience, 2) understand that the past is relevant and gives perspective, 3) realize that they are not born for themselves alone, 4) develop effective communication, and 5) engage creatively with the mystery of being human.[6]

Whatever next steps those at Jesuit institutions and works in the United States take for implementing further the commitment to dialogue will depend on three important resources: 1) the expertise for dialogue that they grow and maintain at their institutions of learning, 2) a continuing emphasis on formation in Ignatian spirituality and spiritual practice, and 3) the growth and maintenance of the Jesuit model of education in their schools at all levels.

---

1. See Fr. John W. O'Malley, S.J., "Dialogue and the Identity of Vatican II," *Origins: CNS Documentary Service* 42, 25 (November 22, 2012): 398-403, especially 403 in reference to dialogue: "It is a characteristic absolutely unique to Vatican II and the surface manifestation of a deep, corporate shift in mindset."

2. Thomas Stransky, "The Genesis of *Nostra Aetate*," *America* (October 24, 2005).

3. Second Vatican Council, Declaration on the Relation of the Church to Non-Christian Religions, *Nostra aetate* (1965), 3.

4. See Yves Congar OP, *My Journal of the Council,* translated by Mary John Ronayne OP and Mary Cecily Boulding, OP (Collegeville, MN: Liturgical Press, 2012) 640; also see Josef Neuner, *Christian Revelation and World Religions* (London: Burns and Oates, 1967).

5. See: John W. Padberg, S. J., *Documents of the 31st and 32nd General Congregations of the Society of Jesus* (St. Louis: The Institute of Jesuit Sources, 1977).

6. John O'Malley, "Jesuit Schools and the Humanities Yesterday and Today," in *Studies in the Spirituality of Jesuits* Vol 47/1, (Spring 2015).

STUDYING AND TEACHING ISLAM: DIFFERENT EXPERIENCES

Patrick J. Ryan, S.J.

Forty years have passed since May 1975 when I defended my doctoral dissertation in the program that used to be called Higher Degrees in the Study of Religion, under the subsection Comparative History of Religion, at Harvard University. Five of us were accepted into that program in 1968; I was the only one who completed it. One of my fellow graduate students at Harvard, an Indian Sunni Muslim, more interested in the philosophy of science than in religion, asked me at a dinner party whether I was a missionary trying to convert Muslims to Christianity. Another Muslim at the same dinner party, a Shi'ite from Lebanon, spoke up before I could. "No, no," he said, "Pat's a priest the way Massignon was a priest towards the end of his life." I think that was the beginning of my hero-worship of Louis Massignon and my love for the tradition of *badaliyya*, the exchange of prayer between Muslims and Christians who intercede not for each other's conversion but for each other's coming closer to God.

Father Patrick J. Ryan, S.J., is the McGinley Professor of Religion and Society at Fordham University in New York. In 1964 he began a long career as a teacher and academic administrator in West Africa, where he has spent 26 years. After ordination in 1968 he completed a doctorate at Harvard University in the comparative history of religion, specializing in Arabic and Islamic studies. Father Ryan has taught at the University of Ghana, the University of Cape Coast in Ghana, Fordham University, Hekima College in Nairobi, Kenya, and the Gregorian University in Rome.

My dissertation research centered—linguistically, anthropologically and historically—on popular Islam among the Yoruba of southwestern Nigeria, a population about half Muslim and half Christian, all of them decidedly Yoruba. The Yoruba number about thirty million and speak related dialects of what linguists would consider a single language. I first lived in their homeland in 1964-65 and the fact that the Yoruba are both Muslim and Christian—sometimes within the walls of the same family house—fascinated me. They could provide a model for the rest of Nigeria, for the rest of Africa, and for the rest of the world.

I mention where my first interest in Islam began because I find that in the United States today all too many people began their interest in Islam with the Six Day War of 1967, with the oil embargo of 1973, with the hostage-taking of American diplomats in Tehran in 1979, or with the attacks on the Twin Towers and the Pentagon in 2001. Such people have no Muslim friends. Some among them did doctoral studies in political science but did not get tenure anywhere, becoming, as a result, itinerant specialists in terrorism. Like the demons who possessed the Gerasene demoniac in Mark's Gospel, their number is legion—people possessed by what Eisenhower called the military-industrial complex.

I have taught courses on Islam in three settings: (1) at the University of Ghana (1974-83) and the University of Cape Coast in Ghana (1990-96), both public universities; (2) at Hekima College in Nairobi, Kenya, a divinity school, and at the Gregorian University in Rome (1998-99), both Jesuit theological institutions; (3) at Fordham University in New York (1986-89; 1996-98; 2006-today), a Jesuit university.

In Ghana, my courses on Islam were mainly taught to Ghanaian Muslim students pursuing degrees in Religious Studies. Late in my first nine years in Ghana a letter arrived on the desk of the University's Vice-Chancellor from the office of the head of the Supreme Council for Islamic Affairs in Ghana demanding to know why "a Roman Catholic bishop" was teaching courses on Islam, and especially (in the absence of a Muslim colleague on sabbatical that year) a course on the Qur'an. The head of the Supreme Council evidently thought

"Reverend Doctor" in my title meant I was a bishop. The acting head of the department at the time, a cautious Methodist layman, called in the Muslim students to ask them whether they objected to my teaching courses on Islam, and especially on the Qur'an. When my Muslim students found out about the letter from the head of the Supreme Council for Islamic Affairs in Ghana, they wrote him a letter calling him out for interfering in something he knew nothing about—university life. They copied their letter to the Vice-Chancellor and to the acting head of the department. I only found out about the whole incident after it was over.

At the Jesuit divinity school in Kenya, as well as at the Gregorian University in Rome, most of my students were seminarians, clergy, or religious sisters and brothers coming from many countries. Some of them came from places like Sudan and Pakistan where Christians were a distinct minority, not always treated fairly. In my course on Politics and Religion in the Islamic World at the Gregorian University, I had nineteen students from seventeen different countries, none of them Americans. One of them was a Muslim exchange student, a Gambian normally living in Tunisia. All seemed to like the course, but the last-described student was the most enthusiastic of all. In passing, looking back at my years teaching in Ghana and at my one year teaching in Rome, I have found it easier to teach about Islam outside the United States than inside, especially in the wake of 9/11. The recent amalgamation of the Republican Party and Likud has not made it any easier. At least once in my student evaluations I have found it said that "Professor Ryan obviously favors the Muslim students." That is true, but it is because they ask questions, in fact, very intelligent questions.

Islam is not a major factor in the conspectus of courses offered by the Theology Department at Fordham, or at least not after the abolition of the History of Religions section of that department in 1983, the very year I first arrived at Fordham. Thus, there was no way I could be hired in Theology in 1983 and I have never belonged to that Department since then, although I have given a few courses under its aegis. I belonged briefly (1983-85) to the Political Science Department at Fordham, an uneasy placement since I had never taken a single course in Political Science, but the appointment was made for Fordham's inter-departmental Middle East Studies program. I also belonged for a while to the erstwhile Humanities Division of Fordham College at Lincoln Center, and I have also taught a few courses in the Graduate School of Religion and Religious Education, a more pastorally oriented school that is not to be confused with the Theology Department. In my present position, the Laurence J. McGinley Chair in Religion and Society, I give two public lectures a year at Fordham, always on themes common to the Jewish, Christian and Muslim traditions of faith, and I always have a Jewish and a Muslim respondent. A Lutheran minister once asked me why I do not have a Christian respondent; I do not think he meant the question in a hostile sense.

When Fordham underwent its last Middle States academic evaluation in 2006, as the then Vice President for University Mission and Ministry, I managed to get Fordham to commit itself to creating a "Trialogue Center." That Center would be a forum where Jewish, Christian and Muslim scholars could study together and teach together, engaging in "interfaith dialogue" that would have the effect of "creating a richer understanding of religion, morality and ethics," especially in New York City, but also in society at large. Such a Trialogue Center would be able to "establish something that is relatively rare in American higher education: a permanent academic center devoted to exploring the ties among Judaism, Christianity and Islam and applying their insights to the many ethical issues facing our society."[1] Three endowed academic chairs were envisioned for concretizing this Trialogue Center: one in Judaic Studies, concentrating on Rabbinic and later developments in the Jewish tradition; a second in the history of Christianity with a focus on Christian encounters with Jews and Muslims throughout the centuries, and a third in Islamic Studies, particularly Quranic studies and later religious developments in Islamic thought.

Fordham is coming up for its 2016 evaluation by the Middle States academic visitors. How much progress has been made towards creating this Trialogue Center? After a year of interviewing, the Theology

Department was unable to settle on a candidate for a chair that has been generously endowed for Judaic studies, and the chair will now be placed in the History Department. They have, however, hired a young Jewish assistant professor in Theology, who brings great verve and expertise to her teaching. What progress has there been toward hiring a professor of Islamic studies? Theology, having done away with its History of Religions section more than thirty years ago, is not restarting it, but Theology does have a well-published professor whose specialty is Islamic studies, although she is not a Muslim. There are several Muslims teaching in various fields at Fordham, including one tenured in the history of Islamic societies in the History department.

    I cannot forget, however, a conversation I had a few years ago with a member of the Board of Trustees, who was comfortable with the promotion of Jewish-Christian dialogue at Fordham, but most uncomfortable with the idea of Trialogue involving Jews, Christians, and Muslims on an equal footing. Somehow I doubt the Trialogue Center will be created during my lifetime, unless I live even longer than my predecessor in the McGinley Chair, who continued to teach until he was almost ninety.

[1] Quotations from "The Center for Jewish-Christian-Muslim Trialogue at Fordham University: A Concept Paper."

THE CHALLENGE AND THE PROMISE OF TEACHING ISLAM AT A JESUIT UNIVERSITY

Umeyye Isra Yazicioglu

I have been teaching Islamic Studies at St. Joseph's University for six years now and one of the things that I value deeply about being at a Jesuit institution is something that I initially had not anticipated. When I applied for the position in Islamic Studies at St. Joseph's University, I felt a bit uneasy. I was uneasy about the prospect of working in a confessional setting, so to speak—in a place that clearly sides with a particular religious tradition, and in this particular case, a Jesuit Catholic tradition. But then, very quickly after I got the job, it became clear to me that there is something deeply valuable about teaching Islam in a Jesuit University. And how is that?

One major reason I value teaching religion in this setting is that it releases the implicit tension that can be associated with teaching religion. What I mean by that implicit tension is the inhibition

Isra Yazicioglu is Associate Professor of Islamic Studies at St. Joseph's University, PA. Her research interests include interpretation of scripture in the modern age, Islamic theology, and the relation between faith, reason and science, with a focus on the Quranic Theology of a twentieth-century Muslim scholar, Said Nursi. Her book *Understanding Quranic Miracle Stories in the Modern Age* (Penn State University Press, 2013) brings Muslim scholars into conversation with Western thinkers over the implications of miracles. Her other works include articles such as "Engaging with Abraham and His Knife: Interpretation of Abraham's Sacrifice in the Muslim Tradition," "Perhaps their Harmony is not that Simple: Said Nursi on the Qur'an and Modern Science," and "Affliction, Patience and Prayer: Reading Job (p) in the Qur'an."

present in our culture when we talk about faith. It is as if we are afraid to speak too meaningfully about faith—of making too much sense of faith. Marilynne Robinson puts it nicely: "When it comes to faith, there are prohibitions, often an unarticulated kind, that are culturally felt and that prevent people from actually saying what they think."[1] Robinson has been successfully teaching English literature and is known to have a faith background. She notices in her students that "if you are Jewish or Catholic, you can make all the jokes about your mother or the nun, but in terms of saying on one's deathbed, 'What will it mean to me that this is how I would have described myself, how does the cosmos feel as it nestles in my particular breast?', they are completely inarticulate about that."[2] In other words, what does it mean to actually claim affiliation with a religious tradition in the way you see the world? In the way you feel about the world? We can make jokes about religion even when we are identifying with it. But when it comes to articulating what is really important about it, we often remain silent. There is an inhibition.

I think there are a number of reasons for that silence. One of the things is that, for students or for anyone, to be part of a religious tradition often simply implies that one is brought up with that tradition. As a child one was taught—this is what we believe, this is what we practice, and these are the traditions. For many of us as adults our religious affiliation is mainly an extension of our upbringing. Hence, it is hard for us to articulate good reasons why we identify with a religion. For many of us, certain questions have never been consciously explored—why do I even believe in what I have been taught? What does it mean for me to be a believer, really, in everyday life, in the way I see and perceive things, in the way I feel about things and respond to things? We remain silent because we do not really know. To the extent that religion is taught like an ethnic identity, passed down the generations as a cultural tradition, it is not easy to talk about its existential meaning for us.

Another reason why we feel reluctant to speak of faith is that certain beautiful things—especially when they are genuine—are perhaps better left unsaid. We may feel that articulating them may be bringing them down. Talking about God and celebrating a world with eternal meaning may belong there sometimes.

But there is another reason for the tension we feel when we speak about faith. Robinson again puts it nicely: "There is an unspoken assumption under the inhibition to talk about faith in a meaningful way. It is as if when you describe something good, you are being deceived or being deceptive."[3] And I think that is a core insight; I see that a lot in myself. Whenever I say something, even in a descriptive way regarding an insider's faith perspective, I have this fear at the back of my mind—I come from a very critical background— am I being deceptive? Or being deceived? Of course, that suspicion about religion is partly justified. Religious people have done silly stuff, oppressive things, cruel things, and they have said things that do not make sense or feel right. So there is truth there, but we also tend to overdo that criticism to the extent that we fail to meet a crucial need in our teaching.

Indeed, we live at a time where there is immense need for talking about religion in a meaningful way. For despite its distortions, faith holds immense promise. I am convinced from both my scholarly work and my experiences as an individual that there is something immensely transformative and precious about religion, at least potentially.

Only religion holds that promise to lift us up from our finite experience to eternity, without which we are just limping in existence for a brief moment before falling into an abyss of nothingness. Only religion holds a promise that can lift one up and say—you know what, this finite existence that you are in, it connects you to something eternal. It puts one in the eternal horizon, and it connects them to something stable, eternal, and transcendent. That is something incredible, despite all the nonsense that religious people do, despite all the criticism that we have to take with all kinds of religions and texts.

To me, teaching at a Jesuit institution releases the unnecessary inhibitions we feel about teaching faith and religion in a university setting. It encourages me to keep the baby as I throw out the bathwater, i.e., to never lose sight of the precious potential of faith even as I recognize the nonsense that can be said and done in the name of religion. Let me give an example.

When I talk about faith in my class on Islam, I try to talk about faith and God keeping in mind that my students come from different perspectives and backgrounds. Most of them do come from religious backgrounds, but by the time you find them in the class quite a few are reluctant about faith. So, I generally explain things in a way that might give venues to students coming from different perspectives. For example, when we were discussing the Islamic creed of belief in one God, once I said to my students, "Let us omit this word 'God.' This word has been used in so many ways that it stopped having meaning for many or has become too narrow. Let us draw it on the board as an empty bubble and then fill it in. Who is God?" (I actually got this idea from a great colleague of mine.) And I explain that to believe in God means believing in something enduring. I gave the example of beauty. Let us consider how we all experience beauty in life, in different forms—from a flower to a mural to falling in love. We also experience ugliness. Now, one may look at an ugly moment or see the transience of a beautiful thing, and say, "This is it, there is no real beauty." Consequently, that is it. There is no genuine beauty for you. For you, this world is ultimately an ugly show, even its beauty is a thinly veiled ugliness because all beautiful things eventually fade away. But you can also say—wait a minute. Beautiful things pass, but new beautiful moments and things keep coming. This beauty all must be coming from somewhere stable. And ugly stuff does not delete beauty; rather, it even enhances it as it enables me to appreciate beauty in various forms and degrees. And so, I believe in a beauty beyond, sourcing these particular instances of beauty and enduring beyond them. And the moment you say that, the moment you believe in Beauty with a capital B, an enduring source of beauty that is beyond all these changing instances of beauty, then *that is* belief in God. I tell my students this is the same for truth, virtue, goodness—if you believe that these are more than just disconnected and vanishing nice instances, and that there is a stable enduring thing beyond these instances, then you are, in effect, a believer in God. This is because the belief in God means to see all these instances in life as *signs* indicating an eternal and stable source of goodness beyond them. This is just an example of how I try to talk about religion in a meaningful way. It is not easy and it takes responsibility and willingness for self-criticism. But we should try doing it, as there is so much at stake in making sense of religion.

In a Jesuit Institution, I feel supported in this challenging task of teaching religion. I walk around campus seeing "For the Glory of God" written in unexpected places like the dining hall or library. Even though many may look at these inscriptions and it may not mean much to them, or some may worry about the dangers of lofty ideas becoming a cliché, it is worth having them. For me, being in a campus that has these praises of God inscribed in places, to have an interfaith blessing service in the beginning of every year, or have graduation ceremonies that start with giving glory to God, means to have a space to honor the immense task of talking about faith in a meaningful way, without being radical or without being narrow—in an open way. I know it is a dangerous business to talk about faith, but this is a precious task that we must not give up trying to do. By the way, let me share an antidote here. I recall when my mom visited from Istanbul, where I am originally from. In Turkey, we have a very tiny Christian minority, so my mother has had little exposure to Christians. I took her to our dining hall on campus and I showed her the statement on the wall, *ad majorem Dei gloriam*, translating it as "For the greater glory of God, Allahu Akbar." Her response was a pleasant surprise: "Really? Wow!" And she added, "There are good people everywhere."

I think that we as Muslims and Christians in Jesuit institutions can work together more closely to collaborate and to enhance the study and articulation of the beauty and reasonableness of faith. I am convinced we should do so despite all our differences. Certainly, there are differences between the traditions. Also, we all know that Christianity and Islam come into tension due to the fact that they are both missionary religions. As missionary religions, they are both universal and target a universal audience, so there have been challenges and competition there. We also have a long history of political confrontation. Despite these challenges, I think together we can bring faith to the table again in addition to the ways in which we are already collaborating.

One way in which Christians and Muslims already collaborate is that they talk about social issues together and discuss how they can do social work together, such as feeding the poor. I think that is helpful, and I hope it happens more and more. Often times in these endeavors there is a sense that, because we have different ways of talking about God in Christianity and Islam, we have to bracket the faith dimension in what we do. Some would assert that we both have reasons to do service for the sake of God, so let's put it aside now. And there is beauty in that unity. However, faith is not something that we, as Christians and Muslims, are supposed to bracket. It is something that we are supposed to explore together and, in doing so, provide a space for people who go through spiritual starvation, which is as important as physical starvation. In this regard, let me note that for many of my students, one of the beautiful things about being at a Jesuit institution is that there is an emphasis on social justice. However, many of my students seem to think that faith is literally irrelevant for justice. Again, while it could be beautiful and inclusive to say that faith is irrelevant to the way you would act with compassion in that it enables the people without a faith affiliation to come and join, it is problematic from both an Islamic and Christian perspective. How could an individual's belief in this ever-present being called "God" not inform or enhance the way one acts in the world? Can belief in an unseen One who sees all suffering, who enables us to feel compassion and want justice, who is just and generous, not affect how you act with goodness and justice, to live more ethically than you would otherwise do? If it can have no effect on your action, is it really faith? As Christians and Muslims, as we get together we need to keep the faith dimension on the table.

I also think it is important for Christians and Muslims today to talk about our similarities. However, especially when Islam is associated with violence, there is a tendency to highlight parallels to Christianity so that people can see Islam in more friendly ways. There is goodness and truth to that. At the same time, I think that we are assuming too much when we talk that way. We are assuming that people are already in love with Christianity, that they are already close to Christianity, and that they just need to see how close Islam is to Christianity so that they can let go of their unfounded prejudice about Islam. However, that may not always be the case. We are living in an age where religion in general, including Christianity, seems increasingly irrelevant. It is important to highlight the relevance of religion together. We have a responsibility as Christians and Muslims to talk about God in a way that goes beyond clichés or mere claims, and to bring out what it means to be a believing human being—how belief connects to the transcendent and how it can shape our perception of ourselves, of the world, and of how we act in the world. This potential for collaboration is what I cherish most about being at a Jesuit university.

1 Marilynne Robinson as quoted in Wyatt Mason, "The Revelations of Marilynne Robinson," in The New York Times Magazine (October 1, 2014), http://www.nytimes.com/2014/10/05/magazine/the-revelations-of-marilynne-robinson.html?smid=fb-share&_r=1, accessed January 5, 2016.
2 Ibid.
3 Ibid.

WHERE WE HAVE BEEN, WHERE WE ARE GOING: SOME REFLECTIONS ON THE PAST, PRESENT, AND FUTURE OF JESUIT/MUSLIM RELATIONS

Paul Shore

Jesuit/ Muslim interactions from the time of the founding of the Society of Jesus in 1540 form a prelude to the current relationship between Jesuits and Muslims as well as those who sustain Jesuit traditions and the Muslim presence on American Jesuit campuses. This journey has been a long and at times tortuous one. Yet there are many reasons to feel encouraged when we see how far we have gotten. The following essay offers a few snapshots of that journey.

Historian Peter Davidson has aptly characterized some of the undertakings of early Jesuits as a "search for equivalencies," an approach that helped shape the Society's contacts with Islam. Jesuits approaching Islam found that monotheism was one starting point, as

Paul Shore has held teaching and research posts at Saint Louis University, Harvard Divinity School, Oxford University, the University of Wrocław, the University of Edinburgh, Trinity College Dublin, and Charles University Prague, and in 2013 was the Allan Richardson Fellow in Theology and Religion at Durham University. He is currently Adjunct Professor of Religious Studies at the University of Regina, Saskatchewan. His publications include *The Eagle and the Cross: Jesuits in Late Baroque Prague* and *Narratives of Adversity: Jesuits on the Eastern Peripheries of the Habsburg Realms (1640-1773)*.

was the shared heritage of the stories of the Old and New Testaments. Yet this search was in tension with the role that the Jesuits cultivated as defenders and promoters of the "Church militant and triumphant" in an era when toleration and acceptance were far from the norm. The result was an engagement with Islam that was prepared at times to acknowledge positive aspects of Muslim cultures and even occasionally to point out parallels between Muslim and Christian teachings. But far more often, Islam was seen as a dangerous rival of Christianity, a "secta" or heresy that had to be combated, one that was associated with the military threats posed by the Ottoman Empire. Stephanus Arator (1540 or 41-1612), a Jesuit born in a Hungarian village that was raided by the Ottomans, could admire the hospitality and standards of hygiene found in Muslim communities while systematically attacking the teachings of the Qur'an. In the same era, a Jesuit missionary in North Africa could write about the "amazing elegance" of the text of the Qur'an as a physical object, while Jesuit communities acquired carpets and other objects such as books produced by Muslim cultures.

On a personal level, Jesuits of the baroque era had meaningful encounters with Muslims, as when Jesuits in Transylvania engaged in dialogue with a Turkish *chiaus* or middle-level government official, or when they debated with Muslim clergy in Ottoman-controlled Hungary. Jesuits operated schools (for Christians) within the Ottoman Empire with the approval of the Porte, although the fathers sometimes experienced expulsion.

When we consider contacts between Jesuits and Muslims during this period, we must ask "Which Muslims?" Jesuit Jean-Baptiste Holderman worked with a Christian convert to Islam in Constantinople to produce in 1730 the first grammar of Turkish written in a Western European language. Johann Grueber journeyed by caravan from China through Persia and Turkey in 1663, and Paulus Beke traveled in the 1640s to Crimean Tatary, one of the Muslim states most feared and least understood by European Christians. In such cases, many of the Muslims whom Jesuits came in contact with would have been members of local elites. At the same time, in territories under Ottoman control candidates for conversion to Christianity included women without male protectors, Roma, orphans, and the seriously ill. In addition, persons recently converted from Christianity to Islam were targeted by Jesuits, as were prisoners of war and slaves held in Christian lands. But few, if any, Muslims were enrolled in Jesuit schools.

In 1579 Jesuits journeyed to the court of Akbar, the Mughal emperor. This was the first of three missions that brought Jesuits to India, where they debated with Muslim scholars and introduced devotional art derived from models popular in Western Europe. Although neither Akbar nor many of his court were converted to Catholicism, this mission brought about a better understanding between Islam and Christianity, an understanding furthered by Jesuit exposure to an early (if inferior) translation of the Qur'an. Jesuits, for their part, translated Bible stories into Persian and incorporated at least one story from Mughal history into their own repertory of school dramas. In the following century, Jesuits encountered Muslims in Tatary, Malta, North Africa, and in the slave markets of the Mediterranean.

In the early decades of the seventeenth century, the Jesuit Ignazio Lomellini undertook the first complete translation of the Qur'ān into a European language that also includes the Arabic text. This translation, although never published, is evidence of the depth of engagement with Islam of which Jesuits were capable, since the Arabic text is meticulously transcribed and the translation itself is very accurate. However, the commentary accompanying the translation continually seeks to prove the followers of Islam wrong—and simultaneously other Jesuits were producing anti-Muslim polemical works that betray a lack of knowledge of the Qur'ān.

Before its suppression in 1773, the Society employed the visual arts, drama, and homiletics to construct images of the Muslim. Typically, Muslim males appear in paintings or plays, although the internal documents of the Society contain a few references to Muslim women and girls, several of which are full of praise. The Muslim men envisioned by Jesuits fall into two categories. There is the minority of "good" Muslims such as the Prince of Fez, who converted to Catholicism. However, most Muslim men portrayed by seventeenth- and eighteenth-century Jesuits possess the negative characteristics of the stereotypical "Turk": they are cruel and morally weak. A painting in a formerly Jesuit church in Győr, Hungary shows a row of anonymous, turbaned figures confronting a raised platform where national saints defend Hungary with weapons and emblems of piety. Both Protestants and Catholics insulted one another with the epithet "Turk," while the alleged sexual crimes of Muslims appear in the internal documents of the Society. As the military threat of the Ottomans receded, these characterizations faded away, too.

The suppression of the Society in 1773, and the greatly reduced material resources with which Jesuits had to work after the Society's restoration in 1814 restricted contacts between Jesuits and Muslims for some time. Later in the nineteenth century, Jesuits returned to regions of the Ottoman Empire where they had been active long before. The twentieth century produced many instances of Jesuit engagement with Islam that reversed the patterns of the earlier, pre-suppression Society. One of the most notable personalities of what may be called the "third" Society of Jesus, which emerged after Vatican II, is Father Paolo Dall'Oglio, who in 1992 established the mixed monastic and ecumenical community of Al-Khalil, dedicated to Muslim-Christian dialogue. Expelled from Syria for his willingness to meet with those opposing the al-Assad regime, Dall'Oglio returned to Syria but was kidnapped by the Islamic State of Iraq and, as of this writing, is still missing and may have been killed.

Not long ago, I visited a Muslim College in Cambridge, England to give a talk on the history of the Society of Jesus, and I was welcomed with hospitality, enthusiasm, and warmth. The adult students I met—both men and women—exhibited a lively interest, not merely about the topic that had brought me to their classroom, but also about the history and variety of Christian traditions, as well as about the experiences of those who study these themes. They also offered probing questions about the relationship between Christianity and Islam in Spain before the last Muslim kingdoms there were conquered by Christians in 1492, and about the role of Christian missionaries in the histories of the Americas. This kind of curiosity, enriched with knowledge, can be a starting point for mutual exchanges with our Muslim neighbors.

The second part of the afternoon that I spent at the Muslim college seemed likely to be more challenging. I showed the class images of Muslims that had been mostly created by European Jesuits in the seventeenth century. These images were not favorable to Muslims: they portrayed Muslims as both threatening and undifferentiated—an anonymous enemy. The class grew quiet; conversation and anecdotes were replaced by contemplation of teaching aids created long ago, in a context of great rivalry and hostility. Not only was this medium of communication non-verbal, but these pictures of Muslims (in this case all male) presented a cardboard villain in the triumphalist story of Catholic martyrdom. Yet even here we could still explore the experience and motives of those undergoing martyrdom. A student commented on the facial expression of one of the martyrs, observing that he seemed undefeated by his ordeal. As our meeting drew to a close, it was clear that the discussion of these hostile images could have been carried much further, to encompass not only the visual cues intended for Christian viewers but also the techniques used to appeal more broadly to human emotion, as well as the relation of these images to the larger body of Christian art. And I should have included the symbolic depiction of "Asia" from a seventeenth-century Jesuit-produced volume in which the entire continent is represented as a modestly garbed and virtuous Muslim woman!

A phrase brought up by these Muslim students, "people of the book," or in classical Arabic, Ahl al-Kitāb, points to another commonality running through all the encounters between Jesuit and Muslim: books. This term was first applied in the Qur'an to Christians, Zoroastrians, and Jews 1400 years ago. While acknowledging that what binds Christianity together is a sharing of the Spirit, something much more than a book (or even books), this designation suggests some of the ways in which conversations among Muslims, Jesuits, and heirs to the Jesuit tradition can be approached. Both religious traditions possess a treasured book that is a source of guidance and inspiration and that shapes their worldview. Jesuits not only have been scholars and transmitters of the Bible, they have also been incredibly prolific writers of books themselves, as a glance at the bibliography compiled by Carlos Sommervogel reveals. Equally, the literatures of Muslim societies constitute a vast and, for North Americans, largely unexplored landscape of riches.

This brings us to questions that Christians and Muslims can address to their counterparts through the spoken and written word, a unit of expression that can be contemplated, compared, and analyzed. What is righteous conduct? How can we communicate with God? How should we regard members of other faith traditions? When should a narrative be taken literally and when can we understand it metaphorically?

The relation between science and belief can be another starting point for conversations. The contributions of Muslim science are well known, and Jesuits have worked both as scientific specialists, such as Roger Joseph Boskovich (1711-1787), and as system builders, like Pierre Teilhard de Chardin (1881-1955). And just as the Muslim scientist Averroes (Ibn Rushd) (1126-1198) was censored for his philosophical views, the Jesuit anthropologist Teilhard was silenced for a time because of his creative integration of philosophy, theology, and modern science. Both men have enjoyed a renaissance and remain influential, not just within the traditions in which they were trained, but throughout the world. The lesson for those of us who seek the best possible relations with the Muslim members of our academic communities lies in the ways these men expanded their understanding of the universe while remaining in conversation with their respective faith traditions.

Respect, hospitality, curiosity, conversation—these can be the keys to the next step in encounters between Muslims and non-Muslims in a Jesuit college or university. Maybe curiosity should come first, not because it is far more important than the other three but because it is a human constant and because it is a motivator of learning and teaching.

Yet with all these possible ways forward, we should not dismiss as irrelevant the distance that has historically separated Muslim and

Jesuit. The faith traditions that each represents both make exclusive and generally uncompromising claims to being the one path to God. The syncretism and comfortable identification with multiple faith traditions that are found for example among many peoples of East Asia are simply not part of the story of the encounters I have briefly sketched here. The very reason that categories of human beings known as "Muslims" and "Jesuits" even exist has much to do with the exclusivity and absolute nature of these claims. It remains to be seen how the American Jesuit college or university, existing as it does in a fluid and dynamic setting, will meet this challenge.

1. Arator (Szántó) Stephanus. *Confutatio Alcorani*. Roma: Instituto Storico della Compagnia di Gesù / Szeged: József Attila Tudományegyetem Központi Könyvtára és I sz. magyar Irodalomtörténeti Tanszék,1990.

2. Bacchi, Umberto. "Syria: 'Pro-Rebel Jesuit Priest Paolo Dall'Oglio Executed'." In *International Business Times*, August 12, 2103. Available online at www.ibtimes.co.uk/syria-jesuit-priest-paolo-dall-oglio-killed-498510 retrieved 29 September 2015.

3. Blanks, D., and Michael Frassetto. *Western Views of Islam in Medieval and Early Modern Europe: Perception of Other*. New York: St Martin's Press, 1999.

4. Colombo, Emanuele. "Jesuits and Islam in Seventeenth-Century Europe: War, Preaching, and Conversion." In *Islam visto da Occidente: Cultura e religione del Seicento europeo di fronte all'Islam*. Bernard Heyberger, Mercedes Garcia-Arenal, Emanuele Colombo, and Paola Vismara eds. Genova-Milano: Marietti, 2009, 315-340.

5. Davidson, Peter. *The Universal Baroque*. Manchester, UK: Manchester University Press, 1997.

6. Du Jarric, Pierre, and Payne, C. H. *Akbar and the Jesuits: An Account of the Jesuit Missions to the Court of Akbar*. Delhi: Price Publications, 1999.

7. Heyberger, Bernard. "Polemic Dialogues between Christians and Muslims in the Seventeenth Century." In *Journal of the Economic and Social History of the Orient* 55 (2012): 495- 516.

8. Holderman, Jean-Batiste. *Grammaire turque, ou méthode courte & facile, pour apprendre la langue turque*. Constantinople: Ibrahim Mu teferrika,1730.

9. Lomellini, Ignatius *Animadversiones... in Alcoranum*. Ms A-IV-4. Bilblioteca dell'Università degli Studi di Genova,1622?.

10. Michel, Thomas "Jesuit Writings on Islam in the Seventeenth Century." In *Islamochristiana* 15, (1989): 57-85.

11 O'Malley, John. *The First Jesuits*. Cambridge, MA: Harvard University Press, 1993.

12 Shore, P. J. Fragmentum annuarium Collegii Societatis Iesu Claudiopolitani: The Account of a Jesuit Mission in Transylvania, 1659-1662. *Reformation and Renaissance Review 8, 1*, (2006): 83-106.

13 Sommervogel, Carlos. *Bibliothèque de la Compagnie de Jésus.* 9 vols. Paris: Alphonse Picard, 1890-1900.

14 Zombori, István, et al. *A Thousand Years of Christianity in Hungary = Hungariae Christianae Millennium.* Budapest: Hungarian Catholic Episcopal Conference, 2001.

ISSUES OF IMMEDIACY AND IDENTITY IN SCHOLARSHIP AND PEDAGOGY FOR ISLAM IN THE ACADEMY

Martin Nguyen

In this brief essay I will address three topics: 1) teaching Islam in a post-9/11 world, 2) the relationship between scholarship and pedagogy, and 3) specific pedagogical techniques that have been developed in response to the first two issues. Additionally, the manner in which I address the first two topics is intended to point out specific issues that we face as educators at Jesuit colleges and universities both inside and outside the classroom. For example, in what ways do the subjects we research shape and inform how we teach? And conversely, how does our teaching inform the trajectory of research and publications? The creative and innovative pedagogical techniques with which I end the essay are aimed at allowing students to experience as closely as possible what Muslims face and confront on a regular basis.

How we frame the teaching of Islam after 9/11 is markedly different than how it was framed in preceding decades. While the change was

---

Martin Nguyen is Associate Professor of Islamic Studies in the Religious Studies Department at Fairfield University. He received a Masters of Theological Studies from Harvard Divinity School and a Ph.D. in Middle Eastern Studies and History from Harvard University. His areas of research include the Qur'an, theology, Sufism, and Islamic history. He is the author of *Sufi Master and Qur'an Scholar* (Oxford University Press, 2012) and is presently completing a book on modern Muslim theology.

well underway prior to this historical moment, 9/11 has become a watershed moment in the collective memory of the American populace. One such indicator of this shift is the rapid popularization of the term *Islamophobia* in public discourse. As a concept, Islamophobia is a relatively new term that reframes many of the issues and challenges explored traditionally through the concept of *Orientalism*. While the precise definition and appropriateness of the term remain an open discussion, Islamophobia has developed into a substantial field of academic inquiry and has become part and parcel of the mainstream conversation on Islam and Muslims. It is now a concept that we have to confront and present to our students. Moreover, when one considers teaching Islam in a post-9/11 context, it is not just a matter of dealing with the events directly related to 9/11. Rather, it entails dealing with the constant stream of crises that continually appears in media headlines. As educators, we must ask ourselves, how do we respond to these issues in the classroom? Should we even respond to these issues at all?

The news events that call us back to this question seem endless. In the first half of 2015 alone Islam and Muslims were explicitly and/or implicitly implicated in a seemingly endless array of media stories addressing such subjects as the spread of ISIS/ISIL, the ongoing Syrian Civil War and the resulting refugee crisis, successive waves of domestic hate crimes, the abuse scandal rocking the Muslim American community in Chicago, and the murder of three young Muslims in Chapel Hill, as well as the gender and racial politics confronting various Muslim communities in the West. How do we respond in a way that does justice to the complexity and nuance that each of these issues entails? How do we work our responses into set syllabi and carefully crafted coursework? Moreover, how best can we respond? We must question what is accomplished by the immediate reaction to be apologetic—typified in that paper-thin argument that Islam is a religion of peace. While the immediacy of such a reassurance may assuage palpable anxieties, such a response is ultimately facile and reductive, if not disingenuous. For those of us who are Muslim academics the stakes feel even higher. While we are trained to be critical academics and educators, many of us see ourselves as committed members of the Muslim faith community as well. This commitment, however, does not imply a position of unquestioning support. Rather it entails our being critical, sometimes sharply critical, of how our communities move forward, develop, and grow. It is a position of criticism born out of deep and sincere concern. On the one hand, we want to speak honestly for and to stand in solidarity with the local Muslim community, which is constantly under intense scrutiny, if not direct and invasive surveillance. On the other hand, we also desire to articulate a productive, internal critique of these same communities that we hold dear. How do we strike a balance as we direct ourselves towards external and internal concerns all at once?

Obviously, the classroom is our first forum as educators. In our carefully crafted syllabi, we often do not have time to address these thorny topics. In some cases, we simply avoid it. With only so many weeks available, we have already whittled down what we can discuss to a handful of key themes and topics. Despite this careful planning and crafting, current events irrupt invariably onto our media horizons and demand otherwise. Suddenly, we must talk about the latest attack, policy debate, court case, or sensationalized crisis. In the spring of 2015, I found myself having to make time to discuss the who and why of ISIS/ISIL in my Islam in America course, well outside of the imagined scope for that course.

The time allotted to our courses, however, are not the only venues for us to formulate a response. The campus affords us many possible outlets. We might consider organizing forums like strategically located teach-ins and university-wide lectures. In these spaces we can do "damage control" for the wider campus community beyond our designated classrooms. Naturally, there are issues involved with these events as well. There is the burden of speaking too immediately or too apologetically. In addressing a situation too quickly we do not allow for all the facts concerning a crisis to emerge. Nor do we allow for sufficient time for alternative analyses to come to the fore. We run the risk of constantly having to respond to the narratives of mainstream media and official government reports, neither of which are unproblematic. Furthermore, whether we like it or not, media outlets are constantly contacting us for our expertise in an attempt to draw us into their narratives.

This raises the additional problem of expertise. While we may all engage in the study of Islam, the field of Islamic studies is incredibly broad. How does specialization in a subset of specific fields and disciplines render each of us into authoritative voices for the news event of the moment? I was trained as a medievalist. I study Arabic manuscripts. What grants me the expertise to speak about ISIS, al-Shabab, or Boko Haram? Nevertheless, our own institutions turn continually to us to represent and speak on behalf of an incredibly diverse and culturally variegated Muslim community. The need to respond to these questions and concerns feels constant in our post-9/11 era.

Tying all these demands together is the fact that time is of the essence. The news fosters a sense of urgency and action. There is the sense that we cannot wait until next semester to organize a proper forum, panel, or lecture—we have to address things immediately. In early 2011 the Arab Spring or Dignity Revolutions unfolded incredibly quickly across the Middle East and North Africa; and we are still dealing with the fallout and ramifications. Our ability to properly plan and collaborate is constrained by the speed of the 24-hour newsroom. In some cases, we can defer to someone else and claim that this is not our area of expertise. Our training more often than not lies elsewhere. Namely, we carry out long-term ethnographic studies; we carefully comb over and methodically analyze texts; we know how to critically interrogate and engage traditions from a variety of nuanced angles, approaches, and perspectives. We are not trained to be public spokespeople or media savvy. Nonetheless, our own universities often turn expectantly to us to fill those shoes.

The argument can be made that we do not necessarily have to fill that public role. Rather than constantly reacting to current events, what we are doing in our classrooms is proactively laying the groundwork for our students to develop a more critical framework of analysis. We are providing them with the intellectual tools to engage and understand the world in an ethical and discerning manner. We help them to question and reframe the stories, narratives, and sound bites they will encounter. All of this, however, takes time—an incredible amount of time and patience. What are we to do with our impulse to put out as many fires as possible as soon as they appear? When fear and anger hang in the air, should we not reach out and ask what we can do in the present moment? Consider the slaying of three Muslim students in Chapel Hill, North Carolina on February 10, 2015. This tragedy viscerally shook the Muslim community at and around Fairfield University. It was difficult for me to take in myself. Nevertheless, I felt compelled to discuss it in my classroom in the days that immediately followed. I was challenged to use it as a means to bring attention to the specific tragedy at hand as well as all the larger issues surrounding it, like race and racialization, the gun control debate, and the growing climate of Islamophobia. The resulting discussions were electric and enlivening. Yet, in order to take this tragic event and broaden it into a moment of deeper reflection for my students, I had to sacrifice what was on the syllabus. In order to address important issues like this, we cannot always rely on our long-term pedagogical plans. The question, then, is not whether to address such issues, but *how* to address them. What is the best way for each of us to tackle these sorts of questions? We must consider what we can address them both, reactively in the immediacy of the moment, and proactively in the long term.

The last point I would like to make about the post-9/11 environment has to do with our positions at Jesuit colleges and universities. We are here to teach. We are here to mentor. Some of us are in positions to help guide students on a more personal level, an opportunity afforded by our belonging to Jesuit institutions of higher education. For many of us, just by virtue of our age we were able to experience life before 9/11 and can recognize its impact on life after the event. We have observed how American perceptions of Muslims have shifted and witnessed how the experience of being a Muslim minority has substantially changed before and after this watershed event. Although the students we face are the same age year after year, we age. Our memory of 9/11 was a lived moment; it is a trauma that we carry with us. When I first began teaching a decade into the twenty-first century, 9/11 was only a hazy memory embedded in the early childhood of my students. Now several years later, our students were mere infants and toddlers on 9/11. In a few years' time, our students will not have existed at all prior to 9/11. At some point in the not too distant future 9/11 will move from living memory into history. This impending reality changes the way we talk about Islam. We have to think about how we are conveying this material, especially if we are addressing Islam in America and Islam in the West in the courses we teach. Our students have a different sense of the past. They have a different perspective on how things are, how things have changed, and how things are changing. How they understand "Islam" and "Muslim" is informed by a different matrix of historical experiences. How can we best bridge this growing divide?

Related to this set of issues is the question of scholarship. As we are professionalized into academics an ideal is set before us: the ability to pursue our research with a certain degree of academic independence and autonomous timing. The demands of the teaching semester, however, invariably alter our aspirations. There is the realization, at least for some of us, that we would also love for our research to be translatable in the classroom and to be relevant to our students. There is a clear advantage in having those two environments, the archive and the classroom, interconnected. Of course, the ability to make and then foster such a connection is not always easy. Perhaps this is a criticism of the nature of the academy itself, but I think that at least for Islamic Studies there are certain parameters—or rather constraints—by which we who teach Islamic Studies are bound. Many of us are trained as Orientalists in that we study languages, focus on texts, and/or write ethnographies. We go out into the field to observe, document, and analyze. For those of us who are Muslim, there is an added challenge. While we go about the diligent, but distanced research that we are trained to do, we have colleagues in our departments of theology and religious studies who are doing directly confessional work. Some of them are outright theologians themselves. They have professional societies like the Catholic Theological Society of America or any number of theological sections and groups at the American Academy of Religion. Our Christian counterparts engaged in the academic study of Christianity are able to pen and publish normative, constructive theological works as part of their scholarship. We are beginning to see our Jewish colleagues do likewise. I believe there is a growing desire amongst us, Muslim scholars of Islam, for our scholarship to have greater relevance and meaning for our faith communities and not to have our scholarly pursuits be seen as irrelevant, inaccessible, or overly eclectic. Can we as Muslim scholars of Islam do constructive theology? One clear hurdle is that there is insufficient structural support within the academy for constructive Muslim scholarship. For instance, positions hardly appear for Muslim theology. Professional societies, publication venues, and academic fora are severely lacking. It is here, I believe, that Jesuit colleges and universities might facilitate the academic professionalization of Muslim theology.

To provide a case in point, I recently received tenure and one of the first things I did was write a constructive Muslim theological work. My departmental colleagues were able to see the value in this sort of academic pursuit since half of them identify as theologians themselves and they understood that my motivation was not only intellectual but also driven by faith. And should not the secular academy make space for this kind of work? Considering that the present-day secular academy was born historically out of a tradition of Christian theological education and has retained space for the academic pursuit of Christian theology, we should ask why could not a similar space be carved out for Muslims within the academy. Would this not be enriching and productive for how we teach Islam and foster Muslim life on our Jesuit campuses?

I do not dismiss the constructive Muslim scholarship that has already appeared. In the fields of ethics, Qur'anic hermeneutics, feminist theology, gender studies, postcolonial studies, and comparative theology we are seeing Muslim academics discussing issues of incredible relevance for everyday Muslims. Significant headway has been made in all of these disciplinary fields. The gamut of acceptable scholarship, however, is still far too constrained. Theology encompasses much more that can further enrich the Muslim theological discourse today. Systematic theology, natural theology, historical theology, dogmatic theology, practical theology, ecumenical theology, theological aesthetics, Hadith hermeneutics, and homiletics, among other possible subfields, remain almost entirely undeveloped. How can such work be supported and fostered at Jesuit colleges and universities that already engage actively with theology from normative and comparative perspectives? How can the structural challenges facing Muslim theology be mitigated as the scholarship moves forward?

Having raised a number of overarching issues in the field in general, I would like to end by sharing two specific pedagogical activities that I have used repeatedly over the course of several semesters. First, in my Islam in America course, I require that students work together collaboratively to design a mosque. The project is incredibly flexible in that it is scalable with respect to research scope, assigned time, and the instructor's familiarity and expertise. With this project the students have to imagine themselves as members of a select Muslim community and face the challenges that go into building a religious house of worship in their chosen location. Students will have different strengths to contribute to the project. Those with artistic and creative inclinations and those who are engineering-minded will make different contributions to the design of the space. Business students, many of whom take this course in order to fulfill a core requirement, can address budgetary and programming concerns and think about the hiring process for the staff. The more literary types can be tasked with writing op-eds in support of the mosque and draft the initial building proposal and mission statement. In these ways the project allows different student talents to work in conjunction. Additionally, it allows students to explore relevant issues, such as the gendered space that we find in mosques, as well as racial dynamics. The assignment asks them to address questions, such as—are we going to serve all Muslims in the community or specific Muslim ethnic groups that reside in the chosen city or neighborhood? To get students to think about these issues more critically, you can stage a simulated town hall gathering or zoning meeting where opponents express concerns from parking to terrorism. Readily available are a host of news articles covering the tensions and conflicts embroiling actual mosque building efforts across the United States. An added benefit of teaching at Fairfield University is that New York City is not far away. My students still remember the controversy surrounding the proposed construction of a mosque at Park 51, more popularly known by the misnomer "the Ground Zero Mosque," and were therefore already familiar with the nature of the protests surrounding that stalled effort. Hundreds of Muslim communities across the country are undergoing similar and relatable struggles. The assignment allows students to connect their learning experience with the local Muslim communities around them. In asking students to think about how to build or renovate a site for a religious community, it pushes them to consider important related questions, such as how we get people to come to the mosque, how we tend to all the many and sometimes conflicting needs of a faith community, and what daily struggles we can address through our specific mosque design. Moreover, the mosque design project does not need to be limited to the United States but could be situated anywhere in the world. The beauty of this assignment is that it can be tailored to many different courses related to the teaching of Islam.

Finally, the other assignment that I regularly use is the recitation of the Qur'an. I ask my students to memorize the very first sūra or chapter of the Qur'an, al-Fātiḥa. Admittedly, the assignment is intimidating to uninitiated students. In this respect, this is a great way to clear the house of students who are not really invested in the course at the beginning of a semester. What the assignment offers is a concerted way for students to interact with a ritual dimension of religious experience. The Qur'an is an oral scripture and there is immense benefit in students experiencing it in a direct fashion. What do the acts of memorization and repetition entail? What does it mean to recite, rather than read, a scripture? To assuage the concern of students, I emphasize to them that the vast majority of Muslims who learn the Fātiḥa by heart do not know Arabic themselves and are in a situation strikingly similar to their own. Moreover, I discuss the pedagogical value of the assignment for each of them. The requirement of memorizing something in a foreign and unfamiliar language requires each of them to discover her/his learning style. Are you a visual or aural learner? Are you listening to the Fātiḥa on repeat on your phone? Are you making flashcards? Are you writing it out by hand? Do you have to reach out to someone already familiar with the sūra to have him/her instruct you personally? While this sort of assignment may not work at every institution, I have found it to be a welcomed experience at a Jesuit one, in that it compels my students to reflect on their learning more deeply. In sum, the exercise brings to the fore questions of formation and discernment.

THE FUTURE OF MUSLIMS IN JESUIT UNIVERSITIES

Thomas Michel, S.J.

I think it is significant that I have been invited to address the topic of teaching Islam at Jesuit Universities from a Christian perspective not so much because of who I am, but because I represent Georgetown's School of Foreign Service in Qatar, the only campus of an American Jesuit university with a predominantly Muslim student body. This past year, I had a total of 80 students in the four courses I taught. Of them, 71 were Muslims, with three Christian, two Hindu, and two Buddhist students, one from Korea and one from China. Before coming to this conference I did a very unscientific survey and discovered our faculty consisted of 23 Muslims, 26 Christians, and six who were neither of Muslim nor Christian background. I say this survey was not scientific because it does not break down how many faculty members are practicing or non-practicing, who among them is deeply committed and who is more lightly committed, and who does not identify with any religious tradition. Last year, I might add,

---

Fr. Thomas Michel, S.J., was born in St. Louis, U.S.A., in 1941. He is a member of the Indonesian Province of the Jesuits. In 1981-1994, Fr. Michel worked in the Vatican as Head of the Office for Relations with Muslims in the Pontifical Council for Interreligious Dialogue. In 1994-2008, Fr. Michel served as Secretary for Interreligious Affairs for the Catholic bishops of Asia and as Jesuit Secretary for Interreligious Dialogue. In 2000 he delivered the D'Arcy Lectures at Oxford University on themes of Muslim-Christian relations. In 2009-2013, he taught Christian theology at Turkish state universities. He now teaches religious studies at Georgetown University's School of Foreign Service in Doha, Qatar.

we had a long-time professor and also a much-beloved staff member who both were quite comfortable about openly admitting their Jewish heritage and beliefs.

I wanted to note the religious makeup of our faculty, staff, and students because it creates a dynamic that is somewhat unique among our American Jesuit universities. Before I went to Qatar, I taught a course on Muslim-Christian relations at Georgetown's main campus in Washington D.C. in which all the students were Christians except for two Muslims. In Qatar, I teach the same course but the breakdown of religious background is exactly the opposite.

Years ago, I was at a Jesuit education conference which concluded that our Jesuit educational institutions should be regarded as laboratories where students of various ethnic, religious, racial, and social backgrounds should learn the art of living together well in pluralist societies. They should be places where we can come to know each other better, face and overcome misunderstandings, study and reflect together on life's challenges, and arrive at deeper levels of interaction and cooperation.

I think that these are the ideals that have motivated those who founded our Jesuit universities in the United States and elsewhere. They wanted to build a laboratory of ideas, a laboratory of encounters, a laboratory where the students and faculty would together be growing through their interaction with one another. That is the way I see what we are doing in Qatar. We were invited by the Qatar Foundation, which is an institution of the government of Qatar, to open a campus of Georgetown's School of Foreign Service. We offer four specializations: international politics, culture and politics, international economics, and international history. Since ours is a Jesuit university, the core curriculum, which all students must fulfill, includes two theology courses; and this is how I came to be teaching in Doha.

Our student body is about one-third Qatari, one-third local students, who may have lived all or most of their lives in Qatar but whose parents are Pakistani, Egyptian, Lebanese etc., and a final third who are truly international, from China to Poland to Brazil and Mexico. Our present student body represents 42 nations.

So what is it like in our little laboratory of religions and cultures? I teach a course in Muslim-Christian relations and we look together at both the history and the current situation of relations between these communities of faith: when did things go well and what factors enabled Muslims and Christians to live and work together in peace? When were the times and places in which tension and conflict reigned, and what were the underlying causes that resulted in suspicion, hatred, and violence? In current relations, each student is assigned a particular country, and they are expected to analyze the demographic, historical, cultural, economic, and political factors that affect Muslim-Christian relations positively or negatively. Additionally, they are asked to review the efforts made to address problems and lay the groundwork for solid relations in the future.

My Introduction to Biblical Literature course is close to my heart. Introduce the Bible to a classroom full of Muslim college students! That class is a teacher's real challenge and joy. I am convinced that to those whose hearts are open to God and God speaking to us, any Scripture—Bible, Qur'an, Buddhist sutras or other—can be an encounter with eternal, divine Wisdom. I wish I had time to share with you all the challenging, thoughtful, inspiring papers my Muslim students have presented on Job, on the Sermon on the Mount, on the formation of the Gospels. For me it is spiritually stimulating to see how their Islamic faith shapes and influences their reading of Scriptures that are sacred to me, and reminds me of the days, 50 years ago now, when I as a young Christian was guided through the Qur'an by my professor, Fazlur Rahman.

But as you know, education does not go on only in the classroom. As we do on Georgetown's D.C. campus, we have an annual Jesuit Heritage Week, with daily activities to study and celebrate our Ignatian and Jesuit history, values, and activities around the world. We come together in student clubs that reflect our common faith commitments—AMAL, which works to deepen awareness of the plight of the disabled; English-language courses for our workers and service providers; efforts to conscientize the public to the situation of guest workers in the country, groups that travel together for Habitat for Humanity or study sessions in a conflict analysis program entitled "Zones of Conflict."

Tragedies bring us together according to our faith commitments. Last year when Jesuit Fr. Frans van der Lugt was murdered in Syria, our Muslim students and faculty organized an interfaith prayer service. When the three university students were killed in Chapel Hill, North Carolina, we marched together in solidarity with the families of the victims. When one of our dorm students died in a motorbike accident, it was a terrible shock for the others, many of whom had not encountered death so close at hand. We gathered and shared our reflections on life and death, and consoled each other, and helped each other try to make sense out of the tragedy.

What is my point in all this? I could have taken a theoretical approach and quoted the letters of Fr. Arrupe and Kolvenbach, the papal encyclicals, and national guidelines, but I wanted to point to some of the lived experiences of our interfaith university community, and I am sure that you can add many of your own experiences at each American Jesuit university. And I ask the question: why are we doing all this? What is it for? How does this fit in with our being Christian and being Muslim?

I think that on one level, we all know the answers and have ourselves given those answers to skeptical alumni, faculty, students, and local civic leaders. We want to overcome misunderstandings. We want to proactively prevent violence in our cities and in our country. We want to fight against discrimination and oppose the marginalization of minorities. We want to show that our community is open to living and working with others. We want to celebrate diversity.

These are all valid goals, but I believe that our motivation for striving for warm relations and good cooperation between Christians and Muslims must go deeper and find its rationale in our faith commitment itself—in our desire to be obedient to the mission that God has given to our communities in this world. For us Catholics, that mission was well stated fifty-two years ago by the bishops of the Second Vatican Council. Admitting that, down through the centuries, there have been many hostilities between Christians and

Muslims, the bishops urge all to move beyond the past and "to work sincerely for mutual understanding, to preserve and promote together for the benefit of all mankind social justice and moral welfare, peace and freedom."[1]

What is going on here? The bishops foresee nothing less than a common mission for Christians and Muslims in our modern world. It is a mission aimed at the benefit of the whole human family and should involve at least four key areas of human life. Muslims and Christians should work together to establish social justice, to defend moral values, to work together for peace, to uphold legitimate human freedom. This is a magnificent vision the bishops have set before us Catholics and one that must be at the heart of our Jesuit universities that are in the service of God, the church, and the world. If we are to be faithful and obedient to the teaching of the bishops in the Council, we must regard Muslims in our universities not as a problem to be solved or as an inconvenient by-product of 21st century American pluralism, but as brothers and sisters who have been joined to us by God for God's own purpose. That purpose is that we Muslims and Christians bear witness together, in our very secular and often self-centered society, to the values that come from God's word, God's message for how God wants us to live. We are called to bear witness to values such as compassion, hope, generosity, mercy, and reconciliation in a world that often scoffs at such principles or characterizes them as unrealistic, airy-fairy, or mere wishful thinking.

---

[1] Second Vatican Council, Declaration on the Relation of the Church to Non-Christian Religions, *Nostra aetate* (1965), 3.

THE FUTURE OF ISLAM AT JESUIT UNIVERSITIES

Amir Hussain

I need to begin with a confession. I was born in a Catholic missionary hospital in Pakistan, St. Raphael's, brought into the world at the hands of a nun, Sr. Elizabeth. Almost 50 years later, I find myself teaching at a Catholic university. Holy Mother Church has a way of bringing us all back to her.

In order to talk about the future, I need to say a few things about the past. I was born into a Sunni Muslim family in Pakistan. As a child, I received rudimentary instruction in Islam from my family. However, at the age of four, we emigrated from Pakistan to Canada. As a result, I received no formal instruction or education in my religion until I was an adolescent. Had I stayed in Pakistan, I would have learned these things (instruction in Urdu and Arabic, reading the Qur'an, etc.) in elementary school.

When we moved to Toronto in 1970, I suddenly became a visible minority, as well as a member of a religious minority. The Toronto of my youth was a place where I was isolated as a Pakistani Muslim. At that time, Toronto was a far cry from the cosmopolitan city that

Amir Hussain, a Canadian Muslim, is Professor of Theological Studies at Loyola Marymount University, the Jesuit university in Los Angeles. He teaches courses on Islam and world religions, and specializes in the study of contemporary Muslim societies in North America. Amir is the author or editor of five books, as well as over 50 scholarly articles and book chapters. From 2011 to 2015, he was the editor of the *Journal of the American Academy of Religion*, the premier scholarly journal for the study of religion.

it has since become. John Barber, a reporter for *The Globe and Mail* newspaper, echoed the sentiments of many of his cohort when he wrote of his experiences in Toronto: "I grew up in a tidy, prosperous, narrow-minded town where Catholicism was considered exotic; my children are growing up in the most cosmopolitan city on Earth. The same place."[1] In 1970, the Muslim population in all of Canada was estimated to be some 33,370.[2] By 2011, the National Household Survey counted over 1 million Canadian Muslims, making Islam the second-largest religion in Canada.

I state all of this to convey that my Islam was shaped by being in a minority context, and so I had to learn about the dominant tradition, Christianity. In 1983, I began my first undergraduate year at the University of Toronto. At that time, I had no idea what I wanted to be when I grew up, I just knew that I did not want to work in the same factories that my parents did. I spent summers with my father building trucks for the Ford Motor Company, and picking up my mother at the end of her shifts from the plant where she worked making fans. Working on the assembly line made me want to pursue any other line of work. However, if you had told me then that I would become a theology professor at a Catholic university in Los Angeles, I would have said that you were crazy. At that point, I had not yet settled on my major (which would be psychology with an English minor), but I had little interest in theology and even less interest in working in a religious institution, especially one that did not reflect my Muslim background. In fact, I chose my undergraduate college (University College) precisely because it had no Christian religious affiliation, unlike the majority of colleges at the University of Toronto.

It was through the study of English literature, specifically the works of William Shakespeare and the visionary artist William Blake, that I first became attracted to the study of religion. You could not, for example, understand Blake's poetry or art without understanding the symbolic world that he had created, which in turn was deeply influenced by the Bible. At the University of Toronto, I was fortunate to be able to learn about Blake from Professors Northrop Frye and Jerry Bentley. In trying to understand in Western stories what

Professor Frye called in one of his course titles "the mythological framework of western culture," I had to learn about the Bible. In doing so, I realized that I also needed to learn more about my own Muslim religious tradition.

At the university, I had the extraordinary privilege of being mentored by Wilfred Cantwell Smith, the greatest Canadian scholar of religion in the twentieth century. He founded and directed the Institute of Islamic Studies at McGill University in Montreal in 1951, before moving to Harvard in 1964, where for two decades he directed the Center for the Study of World Religions. He and his wife Muriel then moved back to their native Toronto where they lived until his death in 2000.

Wilfred's ideas on Islam were shaped during the six years that he and Muriel lived in Lahore, India (the city of my birth, coincidentally), from 1940 to 1946. At the time that he began his graduate work, before the Second World War, the study of Islam consisted almost entirely of the study, by non-Muslim scholars, of mostly Arabic and Persian texts written by Muslims. Growing up in Canada, where there were very few Muslims in 1940, he went to India, which at the time was the country with the largest number of Muslims. This was a revolutionary idea—to actually live with Muslims, and to actually ask them what they thought, and then to actually write about it. But then again, that is what one does when one is the minority; one has to learn about the majority.

They returned to Lahore in 1948, which had, after the forced migrations and massacres of Partition, become the capital city of Pakistan. It was there, in the ruins of Lahore, that Wilfred found his calling, described by Kenneth Cracknell, "so to help men and women understand each other, that religion should never again be used as an excuse for such bloodshed and such destruction."[3]

We Muslims and Christians have been neighbors to each other in the past, and will continue to be neighbors in the future. That is a very important metaphor, being a neighbor. Someone once asked Wilfred, "Professor Smith, are you Christian?" If the question had been "are you a Christian," the answer would have been a very simple "yes."

Instead, Wilfred did what he always did when asked a question. He paused, repeated the question, and thought about his answer. "Am I Christian," he said. "Maybe, I was, last week. On a Tuesday. At lunch. For about an hour. But if you really want to know, ask my neighbor."

Unfortunately, there are Muslims in North America and around the world who have no interest in pluralism. They see Islam as the only true religion, and often see their own particular way of being Muslim as the only way to be Muslim. I will return to them at the end of my talk, when I mention some things we might do in the future. As a teacher, I often have Muslim students who are such zealous defenders of Islam. In hearing their rhetoric of intolerance, I think back again to Wilfred, who was for many of us who study religion, the paradigm of critical scholarship. From his deep knowledge, he was able to offer critique when it was needed. He was not a Muslim. He was not an apologist for Islam. Yet his critique never did violence to what it meant for other people to be Muslim. In *Islam in Modern History* he wrote: "A true Muslim, however, is not a man who believes in Islam —especially Islam in history; but one who believes in God and is committed to the revelation through His Prophet."[4] Those words were published in 1957. In 1962's *The Meaning and End of Religion*, he continued: "...the essential tragedy of the modern Islamic world is the degree to which Muslims, instead of giving their allegiance to God, have been giving it to something called Islam."[5] Those words could have been written today, in the age of ISIS, al-Shebab, and Boko Haram, with equal force and validity.

It is important to stress that there are counters to this intolerance, through the pluralism and dialogue that are also happening around the Muslim world, not just in North America. At this conference, there are so many Muslim scholars doing important comparative theological work in Catholic settings.

In 2007, based out of Jordan, a number of Muslim scholars, clerics, and intellectuals issued a call to Christian leaders with the publication of the document *A Common Word Between Us and You.* That document calls Christians and Muslims into dialogue based on the two great commandments in each tradition (Mark 12:28-32), love of God and love of one's neighbor. In 2008, Saudi Arabia sponsored conferences on dialogue for Muslims in Mecca, and for Muslims and non-Muslims together in Madrid. In January of 2009, I was one of a dozen Muslim scholars from the US and the UK who were invited to a conference at Al-Azhar University in Cairo on bridges of dialogue between the most important university in the Sunni Muslim world and the West. That conference also had Jewish and Christian participants.

Perhaps in the future, we, as Muslims, can help you, as Christians, with a new approach to evangelization, not to change each other's religions, but to help in spreading the message of the gospel, to literally evangelize. We can work together for common goals that we all share. I would be happy, as a Muslim, to live in a land where the ethical teaching was the teaching of Jesus from the Sermon on the Mount. Unfortunately, I don not know of such a place in either Christian or Muslim lands. But perhaps we can construct it together.

We can be seen in conflict and competition, and we have been in both conflict and competition in our history and our present as Christians and Muslims. The Great Commission for Christians and the Qur'anic teaching on *da'wa* or calling people to Islam for Muslims are certainly in competition. It is because of those commandments in our traditions that we are the two largest religious traditions in the world. But we can also be in cooperation with each other, being in what the Catholic Church describes as a culture of dialogue. I have learned the most about Catholic perspectives on this from my friend and Jesuit colleague, Fr. Thomas Michel. About this, Fr. Michel wrote:

> ...the focal question is not whether the church should be proclaiming the Gospel or engaged in dialogue, but rather whether Christians are actually sharing life with their neighbors of other faiths. The basic distinction is not between being a church in dialogue or one that proclaims the Gospel, but rather the option of being a church that is following the Spirit's lead to partake humanly in life with others, and thus constantly engaged in dialogue, witness, and proclamation, or else that of being a church that is closed in on itself and exists in a self-imposed ghetto with little concern for and involvement with people of other faiths with whom Christians share culture, history, citizenship, and common human destiny. When

people of various faiths live together—not simply cohabiting the same town but sharing life *together*—the question of dialogue or proclamation doesn't arise. When they work, study, struggle, celebrate, and mourn together and face the universal crises of injustice, illness, and death as one, they don't spend most of their time talking about doctrine. Their focus is on immediate concerns of survival, on taking care of the sick and needy, on communicating cherished values to new generations, on resolving problems and tensions in productive rather than in destructive ways, on reconciling after conflicts, on seeking to build more just, humane, and dignified societies.[6]

There is any number of future trajectories for Muslim–Christian relations in Catholic universities that I could discuss. In the comparative study of religion, it is crucial that we have our categories correct. Wilfred wrote, for example, not only on connections between the Bible and Qur'an, but more properly between Jesus Christ for Christians and the Qur'an for Muslims or theology for Muslims and philosophy of religion for Christians, or the Christian concept of the Spirit and the Qur'anic notion of God as *al-Hādi*, or the guide. Faith is the appropriate category of comparison in all three traditions.

In describing faith in the Qur'an, Professor Smith wrote:

Faith is something that people do more than it is something people have; although one may primarily say that it pertains to something that people are, or become. The Qur'an presents, in reverberatingly engaging fashion, a dramatic challenge wherein God's terror and mercy, simultaneously, are proclaimed to humankind, whereby we are offered the option of accepting or rejecting His self-disclosure of the terms which He, as Creator and Ruler of the world and of us, has set in our lives.[7]

I do not want to get into discussions of the Trinity here, mostly because whenever I think I understand that concept, or at least think I have some idea of how it is understood, the ground shifts beneath my feet. Recently, I was talking with a theologian who described the Trinity as being non-hierarchical and co-equal, and I thought, are not the terms Father and Son, by definition, hierarchical and unequal, to say nothing of the Orthodox notion of the Monarchy of the Father and the rejection of the *filioque* clause. But in discussions of the Trinity, I do find useful David Burrell's writing on the Great Commandment and the *shema*:

> Christian-Muslim disputations regularly opposed Muslim insistence on the unicity of God to a Christian trinitarian presentation. Yet every student of the history of Christian thought knows that it took nearly five centuries of Christological controversies, plus another century of conceptual elaboration, to hone a 'doctrine of trinity,' precisely because of the *shema:* 'Hear, O Israel, God our God is one' (Deut 6:4). So if Muslim teaching showcasing divine unity - *tawhid* - has been developed polemically over against the 'threeness' of the one God, Christians need to recall how long it took to articulate 'threeness' in God without prejudice to God's unity, so how easily 'trinity' can be misunderstood.[8]

Or, to take another example, let us consider how the Hebrew Bible is read very differently by Jews and Christians. Christians read the Old Testament through the lens of the New Testament, or at least through the prism of the death and resurrection of Jesus. Muslims, I would argue, need to understand both the Hebrew Bible and the New Testament in order to properly appreciate the Qur'an. Certainly the first hearers of the revelation were familiar with the Biblical stories, or else, to take only one example, 5:27, "recite to them the truth of the story of the two sons of Adam," would make no sense. Clearly the first hearers knew something of Adam and his two sons. Here, I make a plea to Muslims to become familiar with the Biblical texts and traditions.

On the Christian side, many North Americans are surprised to learn that Muslims have a long history on their continent. Historians estimate that between 10 and 20 percent of the slaves who came from West Africa were Muslim. Thomas Jefferson began learning Arabic in the 1770s, after he purchased a translation of the Qur'an in 1765. Keith Ellison used this Qur'an when he was sworn in as the first Muslim member of Congress in 2007.

The first Muslim immigrants to North America other than slaves were from the Ottoman Empire in the late nineteenth century and the first half of the twentieth century. Many were itinerants who came to make money and then return to their countries of origin.

Some, however, were farmers and settled permanently. Mosques sprung up in 1915 (Maine), 1919 (Connecticut), 1928 (New York), and 1937 (North Dakota). From the time of the slave trade, there has been a consciousness about Islam in African American communities. Moreover, beginning with early missionary work in the nineteenth century and continuing in the 1920s, there was a specific attempt to introduce and convert African Americans to Islam. Other groups, such as the Moorish Science Temple and the Nation of Islam, exclusively targeted African Americans. When Warith Deen Muhammad took over the leadership of the Nation of Islam from his father in 1975, he brought the majority of his followers into Sunni orthodoxy. Today, the majority of African American Muslims are Sunni Muslims.

In the last half-century, the Muslim population of the United States has increased dramatically through immigration, strong birth rates, and conversion. The Immigration and Nationality Act of 1965 allowed many more Muslims to immigrate than were previously allowed under the earlier quota system. The United States census does not ask the question of religious affiliation, so there is less certainty about the size of its Muslim population. I have seen estimates as low as two million people, and as high as ten million. My own research of America's immigration patterns, birth rates, and conversion rates – similar to those of Canada – leads me to conclude that both of these estimates are extreme. Instead, I along with many researchers estimate that there are between seven and eight million American Muslims.

Muslims are at once a very old community here, but in many ways, a very new one when it comes to building institutions. As a child growing up in Toronto, I had very few Muslim role models. The ones that were most important to me were two African American athletes, Kareem Abdul Jabbar and the Greatest, Muhammad Ali. These days, for young North American Muslims, their Muslim heroes continue to be African American athletes, but also entertainers such as Dave Chapelle and rappers and hip hop artists such as the RZA, Lupe Fiasco, or Ice Cube. For them, the connection is with other North Americans, particularly African Americans, who have long experiences of discrimination and racism that many American immigrant Muslims face.

One opportunity that interfaith dialogue brings is increased cooperation and understanding. This interfaith work also involves the attendance of non-Muslims at Muslim rituals and celebrations and the attendance of Muslims at non-Muslim religious ceremonies. The result is an "Islam" that influences and in turn is influenced by the other traditions with which it comes into contact. As a result of the interfaith dialogue in a city such as Los Angeles, many non-Muslims are aware of some of the basic elements of Islam.

We have welcomed Muslim students into our Jesuit colleges. American Muslims are an American success story, equal in wealth and higher education to non-Muslims. *Newsweek* did a cover story a few years ago on Islam in America, highlighting a 2007 survey by the Pew Forum on Religion and Public Life which found that 26% of American Muslims had household incomes above $75,000 (as compared to 28% of non-Muslims) and 24% of American Muslims had graduated from university or done graduate studies (as compared to 25% of non-Muslims).[9] That Pew survey of American Muslims found that: "The first-ever, nationwide, random sample survey of Muslim Americans finds them to be largely assimilated, happy with their lives, and moderate with respect to many of the issues that have divided Muslims and Westerners around the world."[10]

At Loyola Marymount University we have over 100 Muslim students, who attend because of the excellent reputation for both education and social justice in Jesuit and Marymount colleges. Our past president, Fr. Robert Lawton, has spoken of the value that non-Catholic students (including not just other Christians, but members of other religious traditions, as well as atheists) have in Catholic universities. At the 2008 Mass of the Holy Spirit, the traditional beginning to our fall term, Fr. Lawton said this in his homily: "Non-Catholics and non-believers are not here at the University simply because we need you to pay our bills or raise our grades or SAT scores. We want you here for a deeper reason. By helping us to doubt, you help us get closer to a deeper understanding of our God, this life and this world we share."

Muslim students can help us to understand more about faith, and we should recruit them because they can help us to be the best that we can be.

As described by Fr. Michel, there are a number of initiatives happening at Jesuit universities. In 1995, the 34th General Congregation recommended the creation in the General Curia of the Jesuits of a Secretariat for Interreligious Dialogue. It also recommended the establishment in the Gregorian University in Rome of an institute for the study of religions and cultures, as well as making the Jesuit house in Jerusalem a center for study and dialogue with Jews and Muslims. It was Fr. Tom Michel, SJ, who directed that secretariat. This message of interfaith dialogue continued with the 35th General Congregation in 2008. In 2008, there was a conference on the Common Word document held in honor of Fr. Michel at Georgetown University, with a publication edited by John Borelli. There are a growing number of Muslims who teach theology in Jesuit universities, helping to advance the cause of inter-faith dialogue. One of them, Professor Irfan Omar at Marquette University, has edited a collection of Fr. Michel's essays for a book entitled *A Christian View of Islam*, published by Orbis Books. My friend, Fr. Patrick Ryan, SJ, from Fordham University, is the holder of the Laurence McGinley Chair in Religion and Society at Fordham University (the post previously held by Cardinal Dulles of blessed memory), where in 2009 he delivered his inaugural lecture, entitled *Amen: Faith and the possibility of Jewish-Christian-Muslim trialogue*. Clearly, there are a number of initiatives by Jesuit universities in interfaith dialogue.

As religious people, we may share a common belief that it is our duty to help each other. I am reminded here of a quote I once heard, where someone asked a Christian minister about the quote from the Book of Genesis, where God asks Cain about his brother Abel. Cain responds with the famous line, "am I my brother's keeper?" Many of us adopt that line—that we are not responsible for, and to, our brothers and sisters. This particular minister answered in a different way. "Am I my brother's keeper? Yes, because I am my brother's brother." We have several examples of people from different religions working together to help each other. In Canada, in 2004, we voted Tommy Douglas as the Greatest Canadian in a poll by the CBC (Canadian Broadcasting Corporation). In the middle of our current health care debate, how many of us remember that the reason that we have socialized medicine in Canada is because of him? And it was his Christian roots in the social gospel movement that spurred him. Not that it was his neighborly duty, but his Christian duty to take care of his neighbor. In the current debates about health care and immigration, we see many religious groups stepping forward to help people without demanding to see their identification, as some politicians would have us do.

As Muslims, particularly as North American Muslims, we need to become more visible as individuals and communities as participants in North American life. You, the members of Jesuit colleges, can help us to do this, as we have much to learn from you here. We can increase this participation in a number of ways. We can encourage our children to value the arts and humanities. We have a large number of Muslim doctors and lawyers and businesspeople. Where are the Muslim writers and artists and musicians and filmmakers and actors and journalists? We should encourage our children in these fields, which are of course at the heart of a traditional Jesuit education in the liberal arts. If we want our stories told in the media, we need to do this ourselves. Zaraqa Nawaz has done this in Canada with her CBC television show *Little Mosque on the Prairie*.

Church colleges can also help Muslim communities through the training in Islamic theology offered by some theological schools, a wonderful example of our neighborliness. One thinks of established programs at Hartford Seminary, as well as newer programs such as Bayan College in Claremont. The Graduate Theological Union has created a Center for Islamic Studies, and Zaytuna College was accredited last month. My own university several years ago now admitted its first Muslim imam into our MA in theology. This signals an interesting partnership between theological schools who have the experience and skill to train students for ministry, and Muslim communities who have almost no seminaries of their own in North

America. Muslim communities are asking their imams, who were trained as textual scholars, to serve in roles as therapists, counsellors, social workers, pastors, and chaplains, for which they have often had no training.

As Catholics and Muslims, we need to stand with each other. I offer a plea, here, to speak out when those in your community malign us, just as we must speak out when those in our community malign you. Without naming names (I am a Canadian, and we Canadians are nothing if not polite), there are a number of people in the Christian tradition who have said hateful things about Islam and Muslims. This is particularly hurtful when it comes from Catholics, because with all due respect, you should know better. You know in your history in America about what it means to be persecuted. You know that when Americans first talked about non-white foreigners who came to this country with their strange customs, odd dress, exotic foods, homegrown hatreds and allegiance to foreign authority, they were talking about Catholics, not Muslims.

Perhaps in the future, we can move from disputes about Christology to a focus on Pneumatology, looking at how the spirit of God is at work in the world. I see that in my friend Alain Godbut from Halifax, who is working on a "Nazarene" bracelet to show our solidarity, as North American Muslims and Christians, with the persecuted Christians of the Middle East.

My university teachers about Islam were all Christians: Jane McAuliffe (Catholic), Michael Marmura (Anglican), Will Oxtoby (Presbyterian), and Wilfred Cantwell Smith (United Church of Canada). Of them, only Jane is still with us. It was she who first got me interested in the Christians of the Middle East, and who also got me to do a very different dissertation project, on contemporary Islam in North America.

I was at Notre Dame last week, speaking at the Kroc Institute. There, my friend Ebrahim Moosa raised the idea of an interfaith action circle at synagogues, mosques, and churches. What if on a Friday, we had Jews and Christians circling a mosque where Muslims prayed, and later that evening for the Shabbat services, Muslims and Christians circled the synagogue where Jews prayed. And on Sunday, Muslims and Jews could circle the Church for a Sunday worship service. That would be a very visible symbol of our interconnectedness and our support for one another.

This would be a small step toward repaying the debt we as Muslims owe to Christians.

Many people are aware of the emigration of Muhammad and his earliest followers from Mecca to Medina in the year 622. However, there was an earlier emigration to Abyssinia that underscored the value of interfaith dialogue to Muhammad. The earliest biographer of the Prophet, Ibn Ishaq (c. 704-767), and the famed Muslim historian Tabari (838-923), discuss this migration. As people began to accept Islam they met with opposition from others in Mecca. This opposition turned to physical persecution of certain members of the early Muslim community. Muhammad gathered a group of those most vulnerable, and instructed them to go across the Red Sea to Abyssinia, a Christian country ruled by a Christian king. The emigrants were welcomed and accepted there. Indeed, the Christian king protected the Muslims against demands of extradition by the polytheists of Mecca. The emigrants stayed in Abyssinia until they rejoined the larger Muslim community in Medina.

Muhammad's act represents the first time that Muslims, as Muslims, dealt with Christians as a community. There was no sense of enmity against the Christians of Abyssinia; instead, they were seen as a people that would protect members of the nascent Muslim community. This is a very early example in Islam of the importance of pluralism and interfaith dialogue, and the debt that Muslims owe to Christians.

We can connect with each other in the poetry of our ordinary lives, exemplified in the story of Hagar. Fr. Tom Michel sees Hagar as our "Mother in Faith," and writes:

> I believe that Hagar is a key religious figure and that meditation on her story can enrich the understanding of Jews, Christians, and Muslims concerning the nature of the God whom we worship and what it means to do God's will in contemporary societies. The image of Hagar and her child in the desert is part of today's reality. The low-born, hard-working

domestic laborer, used and misused and cast out by her employers, the single mother abandoned by the father of her child, the foreigner and the refugee far from her native land, desperately trying to survive, frantic in her maternal concern for the safety of her child—this Hagar I have met many times.[11]

Let me end with an example of vision and love as the language of God. As I mentioned earlier, as an undergraduate at the University of Toronto, I had the extraordinary privilege of knowing Northrop Frye, whose last book was entitled *The Double Vision: Language and Meaning in Religion*. In his famous undergraduate course, "The Mythological Framework of Western Culture," Professor Frye would remind us that when the Bible is historically accurate, it is only accidentally so. In the same vein, with respect to the teaching of science in places in the American Bible belt like Kansas, none of my Jewish friends think that the Bible, important as it is, is a very good science textbook. It is, however, much more important than history or science. It tells us about our place in the world. It gives us not facts, but something much more important, truths. Or to quote from Professor Frye:

What 'the' truth is, is not available to human beings in spiritual matters: the goal of our spiritual life is God, who is a spiritual Other, not a spiritual object, much less a conceptual object. That is why the Gospels keep reminding us how many listen and how few hear: truths of the gospel kind cannot be demonstrated except through personal example. As the seventeenth-century Quaker Isaac Penington said, every truth is substantial in its own place, but all truths are shadows except the last. The language that lifts us clear of the merely plausible and the merely credible is the language of the spirit; the language of the spirit is, Paul tells us, the language of love, and the language of love is the only language that we can be sure is spoken and understood by God.[12]

Let us move into the future with the language of love.

1 John Barber, "Different Colours, Changing City," in *The Globe and Mail* (February 20, 1998), A8.

2   W.E. Kalbach and W.W. McVey, "Religious Composition of the Canadian Population," in Stewart Crysdale and Les Wheatcroft, editors, *Religion in Canadian Society* (Toronto: Macmillan, 1976), 221-240.

3   Kenneth Cracknell, *Wilfred Cantwell Smith: A Reader* (Oxford: OneWorld, 2001), 6.

4   Wilfred Cantwell Smith, *Islam in Modern History* (Princeton: Princeton University Press, 1957), 146.

5   Wilfred Cantwell Smith, *The Meaning and End of Religion* (New York: Macmillan, 1963; reprinted, Minneapolis: Fortress Press, 1991), 126.

6   Thomas F. Michel, *A Christian View of Islam: Essays on Dialogue*, edited by Irfan Omar, (Maryknoll, NY: Orbis Books, 2010,), 21.

7   Wilfred Cantwell Smith, *On Understanding Islam: Selected Studies* (Mouton: The Hague, 1981), 122.

8   David B. Burrell, "A Philosophical-Theologian's Journey", in Christian W. Troll and C.T.R. Hewer, editors, *Christian Lives Given to the Study of Islam* (New York: Fordham University Press, 2012), 59.

9   "Islam in America," special report in *Newsweek* (July 30, 2007), 27.

10 Survey available from: < http://pewforum.org/surveys/muslim-american/>.

11 "Hagar: Biblical and Islamic Perspectives," in Irfan Omar, editor, *A Christian View of Islam: Essays on Dialogue by Thomas F. Michel, SJ* (Maryknoll: Orbis Books, 2010), 87.

12 Northrop Frye, *The Double Vision: Language and Meaning in Religion* (Toronto: University of Toronto Press, 1991), 20-21.

www.ingramcontent.com/pod-product-compliance
Lightning Source LLC
Chambersburg PA
CBHW022109040426
42451CB00007B/189